ACCOUNTING

John Eve
BA, M.Ed., FCMA, MBIM, Cert. Ed.
Birmingham Polytechnic Business School

Peter Williams
MBA, FCCA, IPFA, Cert. Ed.
Wolverhampton Business School
Wolverhampton Polytechnic

Oxford University Press

Oxford University Press,
Walton Street, Oxford OX2 6DP

Oxford New York Toronto
Delhi Bombay Calcutta Madras Karachi
Petaling Jaya Singapore Hong Kong Tokyo
Nairobi Dar es Salaam Cape Town
Melbourne Auckland

and associated companies in
Berlin Ibadan

Oxford is a trademark of Oxford University Press

ISBN 0 19 832771 4

Acknowledgements

We acknowledge the help of Marks and Spencer PLC, Southampton City Council, and Sandwell Metropolitan Borough Council for allowing us to publish extracts from their respective Annual Reports.

We are grateful for the help of Carol and Nichola Eve who assisted in the preparation of the text, and Sue Evans for her help in collating the manuscript.

Set by Superskill Graphics Pte Ltd
Printed and bound in Great Britain by
Butler & Tanner Ltd, Frome and London

Preface

This book is part of a series written for students of BTEC National level Diploma or Certificate.

Like the others in the series, this book is directed towards a specific unit: in this case the second year Accounting unit. However, students on other courses should also find the book useful.

There has been an attempt to offer a broad view of accounting by bringing in public sector organizations and their specific accounting requirements. The aim is to offer the student a framework of understanding to facilitate the application of principles to a variety of organizations.

The reader will need to study actively. The activities in this book enhance the learning process and should be seen as essential parts of any course and particularly of BTEC courses.

J. E.
P.W.
March 1989

Contents

Coverage of Indicative Content for BTEC Unit Accounting

BTEC courses are designed to encourage the development of skills in a framework of planned activities that are based on the application of knowledge. Knowledge will be gained from studies in all aspects of business including of course accounting.

The Accounting unit covers a variety of inputs applicable to a range of business situations and a range of business problems.

A breakdown of the Accounting unit is shown below with the relevant block that covers each syllabus detail.

A Record financial information in accordance with accounting concepts

Books of account	Blocks 3 and 4
The double entry book-keeping system, its purpose and development	
Modern manual and computerized accounting systems	
Choice of system appropriate to different organizations	

B Develop and apply accounting concepts and methods to the preparation of financial statements, suitable for different organizations

Final accounts of different organizations	Blocks 3, 4, 5 and 6 Block 7
Statement of Sources and Application of Funds	
Incomplete records	
Stock valuation	

C Analyse and evaluate the financial performance of an organization

Basic ratio analysis	Block 8
Other performance indicators	
Interpretation of published accounts	Blocks 6 and 8

D1 Explain why organizations need financial information for planning, control and decision making

Block 10

D2 Appreciate the concepts, methodology and analytical tools used in the evaluation of financial data

Blocks 7 and 8

D3 Selectively employ appropriate methods in the evaluation of business problems.

Elements of cost and cost classification Absorption and marginal costing Break-even analysis Budgeting Cash and credit control Budgetary control Project appraisal Application of appropriate techniques to organizations with different objectives	Blocks 9 and 10

Introduction

Approach and Method

BTEC philosophy embraces the notion that study needs to be active. Education is more than just knowing something, it should be about using information, applying judgement, and developing skills.

The skills required for the BTEC Accounting Unit are listed below, but it is important to think about the *concept* of skill utilization rather than the exact details listed under each skill.

This book is centred around the need to develop accounting skills. A large part of accounting is concerned with rules, procedures, concepts, and conventions, but it is also very much about communication and people. If full benefit is to be gained from this book, then the skills developed elsewhere in BTEC studies, and in other books in this series, will need to be utilized.

Activities

The book is divided into 10 blocks. Most blocks concentrate on a specific area and cover the objectives and indicative content required by BTEC.

The activities are intended to be integral to the study of each block. They are not assignments and they are not uniform either in style or in suggested time for completion. Some will involve collecting data from sources that exist in the environment, others will simply involve using the text.

Skills

The skills required for the BTEC Accounting unit are concerned with the ability to collect information and to use it in a practical and useful way. In other words not just 'having knowledge' but having the ability to *use* the knowledge in a practical business situation.

Some of the skills are listed below and wherever possible they are practised in the activities that are suggested in this book.

Remember that these skills are important to a whole range of activities in all the books in this series.

Learning and study skills. These will be involved in all the activities and the assignments that you complete. They will be developed as you work on a variety of different tasks.

Working with others: It is a skill to work with other people and to be able to respond to their attitudes and their abilities. Businesses usually contain people who have differing approaches and purposes, and an important business skill is to be able to work with others.

Communicating: It is little use having knowledge or information if you cannot pass it on to others. The skill of selecting the most appropriate method of communicating is important.

Numeracy: The skills in this area are concerned with feeling confident with figures and numbers. Most company reports contain detailed figures for profit and valuation of assets, and the 'users' of such information need to be familiar with the use of numbers. The skill is not just being able to compile statistics and make calculations but also to be able to communicate them effectively so as to convey their meaning.

Information gathering: The business world requires data, information, and statistics. Knowing where to collect the information from, and then actually doing the collecting, is a skill: its development is encouraged in the tasks set in this book.

Information processing: The skill in processing information, once gathered, is important. Processing may mean using computers or other information processing technology, or it may simply mean writing on a sheet of paper with a pen. Choosing the best method of processing is important as a skill, as of course is the skill of actually doing the processing.

Identifying and tackling problems: Problem solving is a skill. Identifying the problem is also a skill. The tasks set in this book will help to identify problems and suggest methods and techniques for them. Being aware of a problem can sometimes be as important as being able to offer a solution.

The skills described above are very active. To develop them you need to be involved in activities and tasks that require you to collect information, use the information, and use a whole range of other resources to aid your studies. This book is one resource designed to help this process.

Links with Finance Book

The Accounting unit is taken in the second year following the Finance unit in the first year. The Finance book in this series has introduced many of the basic concepts necessary for a study of accounting. Reference is made in the text to areas introduced in Finance, but this is quite minimal, so that students will not be at a disadvantage if they have not read the Finance book.

Block 1
The Accounting Environment

Introduction

This block describes the accounting environment and sets the scene for other blocks which will involve you in completing activities related to the production of accounting information.

Reading this block will introduce you to the various types of business organization found in the United Kingdom today. A more detailed coverage of this topic can be found in Book 1 of this series, *The Organization in its Environment 1.*

The Types of Business Organization

Sole Trader

A sole trader is an individual who alone makes all the decisions concerning the running of the business and to whom all profits resulting from the business activities belong. However, a sole trader is also personally liable for all the debts he/she incurs in the course of trading — this is the concept of **unlimited liability**.

The Sole Trader is the most common form of business organization in the United Kingdom. Examples of sole trader business organizations include local retail shops, local garages, and restaurants.

A sole trader may have started the business initially by using his/her own savings and/or obtaining a business loan from a bank. An existing business may have been purchased, in which case the buyer would have paid a price to the existing owner of that business which would include an amount for the customer loyalty that had been built up over the years by the previous owner; this is known as the **goodwill** of a business.

Anyone can set themselves up in business as a sole trader and there are no particularly complicated legal formalities involved in doing so. However, if the business is to be run under a name other than that of the owner, e.g. The Golf Shop, owned by S. Wing, then under the Business Names Act 1985, S. Wing must disclose his name to those dealing with the business. A sign will be displayed in the shop stating that he is the proprietor of the business and all the business stationery, invoices, etc., will not only bear the name The Golf Shop, but will also state that S. Wing is the proprietor.

The Golf Shop

Proprietor Stephen Wing

42, The High Street, Smalltown, Midlandshire ML4 THS

Goods supplied to:– ....

Invoice Number ....

Date ....

Description	Quantity	Price per item	Total

The owners of small businesses involved in certain activities are required to obtain a licence from the local authority before lawful trading can commence or continue, e.g. betting shops, pet shops.

S. Wing, the proprietor of The Golf Shop, may find that the level of sales of golf equipment begins to fall because the local golf course is sold as a site for housing development and people in the area served by the shop take up other sports. He will have the choice of either changing the nature of the business by selling other sports equipment or he can wind up his business, i.e. cease to trade. If he decides to cease trading he will have to pay off all the debts he has incurred, e.g. amounts outstanding for stock, rates, rent, electricity, etc.

If he fails to pay off these debts, for instance for golf clubs supplied on credit, then the **creditor** — a person who is owed money by the business — can apply to the courts for a petition of bankruptcy. If S. Wing is declared bankrupt, his house and other assets could be sold off to pay his debts under the control and supervision of a person, normally an accountant, employed to administer this process which is known as **liquidation**.

Partnership

A partnership is a business owned by two or more people who draw up a **partnership agreement**.

A maximum of twenty people may form a partnership, except in the cases of firms of solicitors, accountants, or members of a recognized stock exchange, which are allowed by the Companies Act 1985 to have an unlimited number of partners.

A partnership may be formed when a business operated by a sole trader expands, and money is needed to purchase more machinery or stock, or to expand the premises. This additional capital may be raised by allowing other people to join the business as partners on payment of a sum of money for their share in the business.

Alternatively, a business may be started by two or more partners, each contributing a share of the capital required to set it up.

In return for the capital invested each partner shares in the profits and losses of the business in accordance with the profit sharing ratios detailed in the partnership agreement. As with a sole trader, a partner in this ordinary or general partnership organization has unlimited liability and is responsible for any debts incurred in the course of trading.

Limited Partnership

The drawing up of a Limited Partnership Agreement allows the partners the privilege of **limited liability**. This means that their liability for the debts incurred by the business in the course of trading is limited up to the amount/limit of the capital they have invested in the business.

Private Limited Company

As a business expands it will be necessary for capital to be raised to finance the purchase of new premises, etc. A limited company can do this by selling **shares**, and the individuals or groups of individuals who buy these shares become the owners/members of the company. These members or shareholders in a private limited company are normally members of one family and as the directors of the company they will also employ people as managers to run the various functions within the company, e.g. production, distribution, etc.

There are two types of share, **ordinary** and **preference**. There is a degree of risk related to share ownership, as the crash of 1987 illustrated. People who buy shares receive an annual dividend which is related to the amount of profit earned by a company. If a substantial profit is earned by a company, all shareholders will be paid a dividend. If the amount of profit earned is small and the amount available to pay dividends is limited, then a preference shareholder will receive a dividend in preference to the ordinary shareholder.

The legal requirements governing the formation of a limited company are given in the Companies Act 1948-85. The first step in the process is for two documents, the **Memorandum of Association** and the **Articles of Association**, to be submitted to the Registrar of Companies.

The Memorandum of Association contains sections which give the company name, the address of the registered office, details of the objectives of the company (the objects clause), and the amount of authorized capital, i.e. the number and value of the shares that will be sold. The final section will state that the liability of the members of the company, that is, the shareholders, is limited. At least two people must sign this document and declare that they wish to form a company. The Memorandum of Association can be described as governing and providing information about the **external** activities of a company.

The Articles of Association contains sections detailing the internal regulations relating to such things as the appointment of directors and conduct of meetings, and can be described as governing and providing information about the **internal** activities of a company.

Details of the directors and the Company Secretary also have to be disclosed and, when all the documents have been approved, the Registrar of Companies will issue a **Certificate of Incorporation**. This establishes the company as a separate legal entity; the members/shareholders of the company are only liable for any debts incurred in trading by that company up to the amount of the shares they hold in the company.

The concept of a separate legal entity means that, in law, the company is treated as an individual. Any contracts or transactions entered into by a supplier with the company are treated in law as a transaction between two individuals, i.e. it is the company that enters into the contract, not its Directors. In law, a company exists as an individual with all the rights and duties to honour contracts for the supply of goods and services, etc. All private limited companies include the word 'limited' in the company name, e.g. 'Replacement Windows Limited'. The 'limited' is usually abbreviated 'Ltd'.

Public Limited Company

A public limited company can offer shares for sale to the general public. Unlike a private limited company, where the shares are held by a family or group of people, the shares of a public limited company can be purchased by anyone. Trading in these shares is carried out at the Stock Exchange, and the price of shares is published in the Financial Times and other newspapers.

All public limited companies include the abbreviation 'PLC' in the company name, e.g. Marks and Spencer PLC. This type of company is the largest type of business organization in the United Kingdom; normally the company has a head office and branches spread throughout the country.

Accounting Information

Owners, directors, and managers of any type of business organization require accounting information. The information can be classified into two distinct areas — information for control and review, and reporting information.

Activity 1

Purchase a local newspaper and locate the 'Businesses for Sale' section. List the businesses for sale and classify them according to the nature of the business activity.

Do the advertisements disclose the amount to be paid for goodwill?

Activity 2

List the accounting information the following personnel will require on a regular basis in order to control the resources of the business organization.

a Sole Trader
b Director of a Private Limited Company.
c The Manager of a Branch of Marks and Spencer PLC

Information for Control and Review

Owners, directors, and managers need to monitor and control the use of resources in order to maximize the profitability of their organization. These resources include stock, cash, vehicles, and employees. Basic control is achieved through the production of cash budgets, sales budgets, etc., and the comparison of actual sales, etc. with the budget forecast. Information is required on the levels of stock held and the amount of cash available to pay, for example, creditors and the running costs of vehicles. The production of accounting information for control and review is covered in Block 10 on Control.

Activity 3 Obtain the annual report of a public limited company and list the accounting statements that are published.

Reporting Information

The owners and directors of an organization need accounting information to review the activities of the business over a time period, usually a financial year. In particular they will want to know if the business is making a profit or a loss.

If a business is in the situation where its expenses are greater than its income from sales or services provided, and it shows no sign of recovery from this loss-making situation, then the owners of the business will have to make the decision to cease trading. It is illegal for a business to continue trading, i.e. to continue to incur debts, when the owners know the business to be insolvent — this is the concept of **unlawful trading**. Information on **performance** is normally produced at the end of a financial year.

A financial year starts on the day a business commences trading. Business organizations in the private sector therefore have different financial year end dates, e.g.

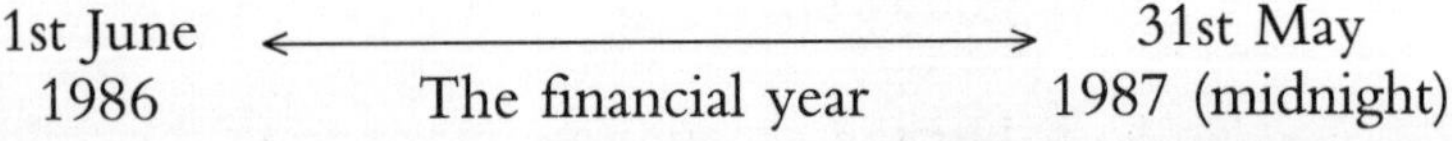

The financial year ends at midnight on 31st May, and the next financial year commences immediately after on 1st June.

Public Sector organizations such as local authorities and health authorities are statutory bodies which were established by various Acts of Parliament. These statutes require these bodies to produce annual statements of account on 31st March each year. The financial year for these type of organizations therefore runs from 1st April to the 31st March each year.

The basic reporting information that is produced is the **Trading and Profit and Loss Account**, the **Balance Sheet**, and the **Source and Application of Funds Statement**. (Check with your findings in Activity 3.)

The Trading and Profit and Loss Account shows for each trading period — the financial year — a summary of income from sales and other sources, and the expenses incurred running a business, such as rates, salaries, and wages. It shows if a business has made a profit or a loss.

The Balance Sheet shows the financial state of a business: It is a 'snapshot' of the assets and liabilities of a business at a particular point in time e.g. midnight on 31st May.

The Sources and Application of Funds Statement shows how a business has financed its operations in a financial year. We will look at this later in Block 6.

Larger business organizations will require reporting information throughout a financial year, in other words the performance of the business will be monitored at more frequent intervals. These may be quarterly or even monthly, depending on the requirement of the owners or the directors of the business. In general terms, the larger the organization the greater the volume and frequency of reporting information required.

Users of Accounting Information

You will have already concluded that the **owners** and **directors** of a business organization require accounting information to control and review business activities. Owners of a business make an investment in a business and expect a return for that investment such as a dividend or a salary. They therefore need to know how much money they have earned or lost from their investment.

The **Inland Revenue** use the Trading and Profit and Loss Account as a basis for calculating the tax to be paid on the profit earned by a business. In the case of a sole trader or partnership, **income tax** is paid by the sole trader or partners on the profits earned in a financial year. A limited company will be assessed as an individual entity and the company will have to pay **corporation tax** on the profits earned in a financial year.

Employees of a business organization will be interested in the end-of-year results, particularly if the organization runs an employee profit-sharing scheme, or if a profit-related bonus is paid to employees. Future employment prospects are also related to the profitability of an organization. If the level of sales in a business has been dropping for a number of years, and the profit levels have also been dropping, then it is inevitable that some time in the future there will be job losses in order to cut costs, or the business may even cease to trade.

Potential creditors of a business — individuals or companies who supply goods or services to a business on credit — will often require assurances about the ability of a business to pay its debts. They will therefore often wish to consult recent Balance Sheets before entering into a contract for the supply of goods or services; they will want to ensure as far as possible that the business they supply will be able to pay the debt at a later date.

Existing creditors will be interested in the financial state of a customer, particularly in their ability to pay any existing debts outstanding. The existing creditor will also be looking for continuing ability to pay debts for any future supplies of goods or services.

Banks and other institutions who are asked by a business to provide loans or overdraft facilities will use the financial statements produced by an organization as a basis for making their decision. The accounting statements for a number of years will be analysed in order to gauge the ability of the business to repay the loan or overdraft facility.

Summary

This block covered, in general terms, the scope of accounting. Accounting is the activity of recording transactions and producing statements not only for business organizations operated for profit, but for all organizations however structured.

Local authorities, colleges, hospitals, charities, sports associations, and in fact any other organizations that you can think of will need to record their transactions and then summarize them in the form of accounting statements.

The block that follows contains interviews with people who either prepare or use accounting information. Try to think of the differences between the roles of the interviewees and also think of the similarities.

Different businesses may well require different styles of information, but essentially the need for accurate recording of events is the same for each. Similarly the owners of all businesses need information about the success of the business, and accounting information provides this.

Block 2
The Producers and Users of Accounting Information

Introduction

This block contains interviews with people involved in accounting. It will introduce you to the various personnel involved in the production and use of accounting information. It will also give you an insight into the variety of tasks that have to be carried out in the accounting environment in order to produce accurate accounting information for use in an organization.

1 *The Sole Trader*

I own and run 'The Golf Shop' which is located in a small town in the Midlands.

I won some money on the football pools two years ago, and as I have always played golf — I was a national junior champion — I decided to use the money I had won to set up my own business selling golfing and other sports equipment. I rent the shop and run the business on my own. I am in the position at present where the income from sales is just covering the expenses of rent, rates, electricity, and insurance. I have only just started drawing some money out of the business for my own personal use; up until now I have been living off the remainder of my pools win and my savings.

At this time therefore, I cannot afford to employ any staff to help me in the shop or to keep a record of the financial activities of my business. A lot of small businesses employ part-time staff to help run the business. Most employ a part-time **book-keeper**, a person who maintains the accounting records for them.

I maintain my own accounting records. When I started the business I had no idea at all about book-keeping so I enrolled on a short course at the local college of further education called 'Book-Keeping for a Small Business'. This course introduced me to the basic concepts and practice of **book-keeping**. We then went on to learn how to use the various book-keeping packages that are available for use on micro-computers.

You have probably realized that things are a bit tight financially, so I cannot afford to maintain my accounting records using a computer. Instead I purchased some hard-back books from Smiths in which I maintain my accounts using the **double entry system** I learnt on the course.

The book is called a **ledger** and I have divided it up into sections in which I maintain the various accounts.

I have a **receipting machine** (most people call it a 'cash till'). I always keep a small float of £50 in change in the till drawer. When I make a cash sale, I key in the amount of the sale and this is recorded on a **tally roll** inside the machine. The amount is also recorded on a **receipt roll**; the printed receipt that is produced is given to the customer. At the end of each day I operate a **total mechanism** on the machine and the till display shows the total amount collected, this total amount is also recorded on the tally roll. I then count the cash and cheques in the till drawer and see if the total, less the £50 float I started with, agrees with the amount on the till display.

At the end of each working day I record the amount of these takings in the section of the ledger in which I maintain the **Cash Account**. This account, like all other accounts in the ledger, is divided into two halves, the **debit** side and the **credit** side. I write the total amount of takings for each working day on the debit side, that is, the left hand side of the Cash Account.

So that I know how much golfing equipment I have sold, I maintain a **Sales Account** in another section of the ledger. I credit this account with the total amount of takings for each day, ie, on the right hand side of the Sales Account. This is the **opposite** entry to the amount recorded in the **Cash Account**.

On some days I do not bank all the cash and cheques I have obtained from Sales — I buy some stocks of golfing and other sports equipment for cash or purchase some small items of stationery, till rolls for instance. I record these payments on the credit side of the Cash Account.

I record the amount of cash I spend buying golfing and other sports equipment from the manufacturers or suppliers on the debit side of a **Purchases Account** and I debit the appropriate Expense Account with the amount I spend on such things as stationery. The Stationery Account is just one of the variety of expense accounts.

I keep the Cash, Sales, Purchases, and Expense Accounts in separate sections of the ledger. It took me a long time to grasp the idea of **double entry book-keeping**. I kept getting my debits and credits mixed up. All I do now is remember that a debit entry, or entry on the left-hand side of an account, represents an inflow into the business, a receipt of cash or the purchase of stock or stationery for instance. The credit entry, or entry on the right-hand side, represents an outflow from the business, such as the payment of cash to manufacturers or suppliers for stocks of golfing equipment.

When I purchase some goods on credit, I record the amount of the purchase on the debit side of the Purchases Account and credit what is known as a **Personal Account** in the name of the **creditor**. I maintain a Personal Account for each individual creditor in a separate section in the ledger. In the same way if I sell some goods on credit, I record the amount of the sale or the credit side of the Sales Account and open a Personal Account in the name of the **debtor**. Again I maintain a Personal Account for each individual debtor in a separate section in the ledger.

My creditors usually allow me a twenty-eight day credit period. When I pay a creditor, I credit the Cash Account and debit the appropriate creditor's Personal Account. In the same way when I receive money from a debtor, I debit the Cash Account and credit the appropriate debtor's Personal Account.

At the end of each month I balance off the accounts in the ledger, that is, I add up each side and carry forward the balancing figure as appropriate. As I run the business and keep the books, I always have a rough idea of how much I owe my creditors and how much I am owed by my debtors. At the end of each month, using the figures from the accounts, I can calculate the exact amounts owing to and from my creditors and debtors, the total sales and purchases I have made, and the expenses I have incurred.

At the end of my first year of trading I had to find myself an accountant to check my books and to draw up for me a

Trading and Profit and Loss Account and a **Balance Sheet**.

A friend of mine, who plays a good round of golf, recommended an accountant called Mrs Wright, one of the partners in a firm of Chartered Accountants — Addup, Checkum, and Correct who have an office at the other end of the High Street. I took my ledger, till rolls, cheque book stubs, bank paying-in books, bank statements, invoices, and receipts to her and made an appointment to see her two weeks later.

When I arrived for my appointment, Mrs Wright gave me a folder which contained a Trading and Profit and Loss Account for my first year of trading, and a Balance Sheet showing my financial position on the last day on that year. She had signed a certificate which was attached to the accounts stating that she had prepared the accounts from the books and records presented to her, and that in her opinion they gave a **true and fair view** of the financial affairs of my business for that financial year. Apparently the Inland Revenue will not accept accounts unless they have this certificate attached to them which has been signed by a **practising accountant**. I think that means they have to be qualified and hold a **practising certificate**.

I spent about an hour with Mrs Wright discussing how my business was progressing. She also offered me advice on the payment of tax on the profits earned by the business and how to complete my tax return. She said it was all part of the service and included in the fee.

2 *A Book-Keeper in a Public Limited Company*

The company I work for manufactures aero and marine engines and is organized on the basis of seven divisions. I work in the Civil Aero Engine Division which manufactures aero engines and supplies spare parts.

I have worked in this division for thirty years now and in that time I have seen a drastic change in the way accounting records are maintained. As well as the training I received working as a Junior Accounts Clerk in this Division's Accounts Department, I also studied for the London Chamber of Commerce book-keeping examination by correspondence course.

On completion of my training which lasted about three years, I was appointed as an Accounts Clerk in the Division's Accounts

Department. There are twenty staff in this department who are responsible for the maintenance of all accounting records relating to the Division and the production of regular summary accounting statements, costs statements, and reports. These are passed to the Division Accountant who produces monthly accounting statements which he presents to the Financial Director of the Company.

When I first started working in this Department, all financial transactions were recorded manually in two books, the **Cash Book** and the **Ledger**. Over the years, however, the volume of financial transactions became so large that we were maintaining many thousands of separate accounts and it became necessary to split the ledger up and separate ledgers were introduced for Sales and Purchases.

I was appointed as the Sales Ledger Clerk ten years ago. The ledger I maintain does not contain the Sales Account; this is maintained in the General Ledger. My job is therefore to maintain all our customers' personal accounts in the Sales Ledger.

The Sales Department sends me a copy of every invoice they raise for sales on credit, and I record the transaction by making a debit entry in the customer's personal account. Payments are received by the Cashiers Department and each day I receive a list of all payments received, signed by the cashier. I credit the appropriate personal account to record the payment by the customer.

At the end of each month I balance off the accounts and calculate the amounts owed by each customer. Each customer is sent a statement at the end of every month which details the invoices rendered and the payments received. I am responsible for the accuracy of these statements and for calculating the total debtors figure at the end of a month. I prepare a list of the debts outstanding at the end of every month and pass them to the Division Accountant.

As well as my book-keeping duties I have to answer queries from the Sales Department, or direct from customers, relating to invoices outstanding, discounts, and adjustments.

The Company Directors recently decided that all accounting systems should be computerized, and at present we are in the process of transferring all records from the various ledgers to a micro-computer. The company's Computer Department has produced the book-keeping software system which is just part of the company's new computerized accounting system. My sales ledger system **interfaces** with other systems within the company, such as the stock control system; to enable efficient stock management.

The new computerized system means that instead of manually writing in each transaction, I now key in the details of the transaction and the computer records the entry in the appropriate account.

At the end of each month I key in the 'balancing off' commands, and the system produces a list of outstanding amounts and statements for each individual debtor. This new system certainly saves a lot of time, and some activities now only take minutes instead of hours. I suppose I will soon be given other accounting duties to fill in the spare time I now have!

Activity 1

Look through the last few editions of your local newspaper and find an advertisement for a book-keeper. What type of business organization is advertising for a book-keeper and what salary is offered?

Do book-keepers need any particular qualifications before they can apply for a position in a business organization, or is experience and adaptability the essential requirement?

3 *Certified Accountant in a Public Limited Company*

I left school when I was eighteen years old and immediately joined this company as a trainee accountant. I studied for five years at a local polytechnic on a day release course. The subjects included financial accountancy, management accountancy, company law, auditing, taxation, and financial management. I was admitted as a member of the Chartered Association of Certified Accountants when I had passed the three stages of qualifying examinations set on the various subjects I had studied on the course.

On qualification I was appointed as Assistant Divisional Accountant in the Civil Aero Engine Division, one of seven divisions making up the company.

I am responsible for the control and supervision of all the staff in the Accounts Department and for ensuring that the accounting systems operate effectively and that accurate accounting information is produced. I have to ensure that we have sufficient staff within the department who are capable of fulfilling the numerous accountancy activities. I have to ensure that all staff receive adequate training; recently I have organized training programmes for all staff as part of the company's policy of computerizing all accounting systems. These programmes have covered such topics as keyboard familiarization and security of information stored on disk.

A regular monthly task that I have to complete is the production of Divisional Accounting Statements for the Financial Director. These monthly statements are analysed and discussed by the Board of Directors and decisions are made regarding such things as stock levels, production targets, and selling prices. It is important therefore that these statements are produced on time and contain relevant and accurate information.

In order to produce these statements, I receive information from various staff in the Department relating to numerous items including purchases, sales, and bank balances. From this information I draw up a Trading Statement for the month and prepare a projected cash flow forecast for the next month. I have to monitor the level of cash and bank balances on a daily basis to ensure the company has sufficient funds available to meet our creditor payments and other expenses.

If we need temporary overdraft facilities, I agree these with the local bank manager after consultation with the Financial Director. In order to keep the amount of money overdrawn to a minimum, and therefore reduce the interest charges on the overdraft, I have to continuously monitor our debt collection system to ensure that money is collected from customers quickly. I also ensure that creditors are paid within the allowed credit period, in order to take full advantage of any early settlement discounts which are offered.

When the statements are complete I inform the **external auditors** of the company, Addup, Checkum, and Correct, who send a team of **auditors** in to carry out an **audit** of the Accounting Statements I have prepared. The auditors check all the supporting records within each division from which the figures included in the accounting statements are calculated, and also physically **verify** the existence of the various **assets**, such as equipment and machinery, which are included in the **Balance Sheet**.

I have to ensure the auditors have access to all information and that the appropriate staff member is available to answer any queries they may have. When the auditors are satisfied that the information is correct, the partner in the firm responsible for the audit signs a certificate to say that in their opinion the accounts give a true and fair view of the financial affairs of the company.

There is keen competition now between public limited companies regarding the presentation of their annual reports and we have attempted to make ours the most attractive and **readable** in the Country. We were awarded second slot recently in a survey carried out by an Accounting Journal which is promoting the need for limited company Annual Reports to be colourful, informative, and readable for all sections of the community.

Activity 2

Obtain the Annual Report of a public limited company of your choice. Find the following:
a The Profit and Loss Account
b The Balance Sheet
c The Auditors' Certificate

What other information is contained in the Annual Report to support the accounting statements?

4 *A Management Accountant in a Public Limited Company*

I left college with a BTEC Higher National Diploma in Business and Finance and joined this company as a Trainee Management Accountant. My diploma gave me some exemptions from the subjects I had to study on a course provided by a local College of Higher Education. After three years of study I had passed all the examinations which qualified me for membership of the Chartered Institute of Management Accountants.

I have been employed by this company for over thirteen years now and recently I was promoted to the position of Chief Management Accountant in the Civil Aero Engine Division. There are three qualified and four part-qualified management accountants in the Management Accountancy Section of the Accounts Department. I am responsible for the work of the section, which is to provide management accounting information to all departments within the division. There are two functions carried out by the section, these are **costing** and the provision of **management information**.

Costing involves the preparation of detailed cost statements for departments, operations, and products. If the company is considering launching a new product it would be my responsibility to provide a detailed analysis of the cost of producing that product. All the various **cost elements** would have to be identified and the **production cost** of the product calculated. A decision would then have to be made as to the **selling price** of the product based on the production cost plus a percentage **profit** in relation to sales forecasts.

Management accounting therefore involves the analysis of costs and the provision of information to managers as a basis for decision making.

The main work carried out by this section is the production of monthly or weekly cost statements for the managers of the various departments or operations within the division. For example, each month we produce a cost statement for the Stores Manager in the division. The information provided in the statement details the value of parts issued from the stores and the cost of running the stores, split between **fixed** and **variable costs**. Fixed costs include rates and insurance, and variable costs include the wages paid to the storeman and the cost of telephone calls. From this information we can calculate the cost of issuing each individual item from the stores.

Managers need information on the costs of running their departments or operations in order to monitor and control costs. The basis of cost control within the division is the **budget**. Budgets are prepared which detail the estimated costs for a financial year of running a department or operation. It is against the **budgeted costs** that **actual costs** are compared as a basis for monitoring and control. This section is responsible for the preparation of the budgets for all departments and operations within the company. Each year, information is produced relating to the sales targets for the next financial year. A budget is prepared for the next financial year based on the production levels and support operations required to produce and deliver the goods in relation to the sales target. Individual budgets are prepared for purchasing, production, storage, and sales.

As you can imagine, the volume of data required to produce detailed budgets for each department or operation is massive. All budgets are now prepared using micro-computers; we have developed detailed budgets based on the information keyed in by members of my section. The computer system also provides data as a basis for our **budgetary control system**.

Each department or operation is classified as a **cost centre** and the computer system matches expenditure or income coded to a particular cost centre. By keying in the appropriate commands we can produce a print-out either weekly or monthly which compares actual and budgeted costs, showing us any **variance**. A variance can be **favourable**; that is expenditure is less than budgeted or income more than budgeted, or **adverse**; that is expenditure is greater or income is less than budgeted.

Departmental or Operations Managers are sent weekly or monthly **budgetary control reports** which summarize the figures and highlight the variances. Variances have to be explained by managers and very often we are involved in discussions with managers on ways of improving or rectifying adverse variances. This could mean a change in production or working methods. Of course no definite decisions are taken before consulting senior management and other concerned parties such as trade unions.

Another aspect of my work is to ensure that costs are kept to a minimum. **Variable overheads**, such as wages, need careful monitoring and control. In some areas I monitor cost levels with a view to cutting them in order for a particular department or operation to become more profitable. These **cost reduction** exercises can range from reducing the number of hourly paid employees to changing production methods in order to reduce overhead costs.

This section also maintains a computer-based stock accounting system which records all items of stock, the cost price, and current stock held. This system interfaces with the Sales Department computer system, and as sales are recorded, the stock records are updated accordingly. This system is the basis of our stock control system and this section has to monitor stock levels and turnover as well as carrying out random physical stock counts to ensure the figures recorded are correct.

At the end of each financial year we have to organize a physical stock count and calculate the value of raw material stocks, work-in-progress, and finished goods. This information is passed on to the Parts Division Accountant who is responsible for the production of the Company's Annual Report.

5 *A Chartered Accountant in Private Practice*

I left University with a second class honours degree in Accounting and joined this practice, Addup, Checkum, and Correct as a trainee accountant. My degree gave me exemption from part 1 and some of part 2 subjects of the three-part professional examinations of the Institute of Chartered Accountants. The course of study I undertook was provided by a private tuition college and involved distance learning packages and some full-time attendance.

I completed the examinations eight years ago and was admitted as a qualified member of the Institute of Chartered Accountants. During my training I spent one year in each of the three sections of the practice and gained experience in all aspects of accounting work within a private practice. After qualification I worked as an accountant in the Small Business Section of the practice and last year was appointed as a **partner** with specific responsibility for that section. As a partner I am a member of the firm's management team. In addition to my salary I receive a share of the annual profits made by the practice.

The practice is split into three sections, Small Business, Personal Taxation and Finance, which includes Executorship, and a Companies Section which is responsible for the external audit of a number of large companies in the area.

In my section there are three qualified accountants, three trainee accountants, two accounts clerks, and two word processor operators.

Individuals or groups of individuals who are considering setting up a small business will come to this practice for advice regarding the formation of the business and the raising of capital required to establish the business and commence trading. Members of staff in this section can advise them on the various sources of funds available such as government grants and business loans and on all aspects of running a small business from marketing a product to the maintenance of accounting records.

The main work carried out by this section involves the preparation of **Trading and Profit and Loss Accounts** and **Balance Sheets** for numerous small businesses as well as the completion of **value added tax returns** and advice on **taxation**. The Inland Revenue will only accept accounts from small businesses that are signed by a practising accountant, that is, by an accountant who has been issued with a practising certificate by their professional body (in my case the Institute of Chartered Accountants).

Each accountant within my section is allocated a workload of clients. As well as being the manager of my department, which involves supervision of staff, I have to sign accounts and VAT returns, and in addition I have my own workload of clients, many of whom I have known since I started as a trainee in the practice.

The best way to explain the work I carry out is to describe the events of a typical week:

Monday: I meet a client who is considering expanding his existing business. We discuss the performance of his business over the past few years and the prospects for the future. I arrange to visit his business next week at the same time as his bank manager in order to look at the scale of his present operations and the plans for expansion.

It takes me the rest of the morning to check the Trading and Profit and Loss Account and Balance Sheet for 'The Golf Shop'. I have not personally prepared the accounts, this has been done by one of the trainee accountants in my section, but it is my responsibility to check the accounts and sign the certificate attached to them which gives my **opinion** on their truth and fairness.

The afternoon is spent discussing and working through all the records of a business with one of the trainees. The task of compiling the accounts has proved particularly difficult as no formal book-keeping system has been used. The only basis available for the preparation of the accounts has been the bank statements, till rolls, and invoices. We had to make decisions regarding **depreciation** of assets and the level of provision required for **bad debts**.

Tuesday: I attend a conference called 'Update on Taxation' organized by the Institute and held in London. I regularly attend courses and conferences on accounting matters, including computing and taxation, and this helps to update my knowledge. I see it as part of my continuing professional education.

Wednesday: I spend the first part of the morning making a number of telephone calls, and the remainder with the owner of 'The Golf Shop'. We discuss the accounts for his first year of trading and I also explain aspects of personal taxation in relation to his drawings from the business. It is usually the allowances that can be claimed that proves to be the most interesting part of the discussion.

I spend the afternoon discussing problems encountered by members of staff in my section and plan the various jobs to be completed over the next two weeks. The partner with responsibility for the Personal Taxation and Finance Section is off sick and I have to see one of his clients who is very upset because he has lost a substantial sum of money in the recent stock market crash.

Thursday: One of the other accountants and I spend all morning with two clients who have formed a partnership to set up a small manufacturing business. We have compiled some accounts for their first six months of trading and discussions are held concerning past performance and future prospects. They are having particular problems with cash flow and some creditors are threatening to take legal action to recover the money owed to them. We analyse their expected sales and expenditure levels for the next six months and prepare a **Cash Flow Forecast**. It is decided that negotiations should be held with their bank manager to arrange overdraft facilities to allow urgent payments to be made to creditors.

I have a working lunch with the owner of a local restaurant who is considering expansion, and spend the afternoon checking and signing accounts and VAT returns.

Friday: One of my responsibilities in the practice is training. I have organized a training session on VAT for all of the trainees in the practice. I give a lecture for an hour, and this is followed by exercises for the trainees to complete. We then discuss the results as a group.

Friday afternoon is the traditional time for holding partners' meetings. We discuss the workload of the various sections, the performance of various members of staff, and plans to expand the work of the practice, which include the purchase of empty premises next door.

As you can see, the work is interesting and varied. Most of the preparation of accounts is carried out on micro-computers, so the traditional image of a chartered accountant is rapidly changing.

I need to develop and maintain good working relationships with other professions and institutions such as solicitors, bank managers, and estate agents in order to provide a source of finance and advice for our clients.

6 *An Accounting Technician in a Local Authority*

I left school with eight GCE 'O' levels and was appointed as an accounts clerk with the County Council in the Treasurer's Department. I was employed initially in the wages section where I was responsible for the routine clerical duties involved in the payment of wages to catering staff in local primary schools.

I soon realized that if I wanted to advance within the organization and make a career for myself in the department, I would have to study for an accounting qualification. As I only had 'O' levels, I was advised by the Deputy Treasurer, who is responsible for training, to enrol on a two-year day release course at the local technical college to study for a BTEC National Certificate in Business Studies. On completion of this course, I had to attend another course for a further year at the same college on a day release basis to prepare me for the examinations which qualified me for membership of the Association of Accounting Technicians.

The Council was very generous during my training period and allowed me to attend the day release course without loss of pay, and they also paid my tuition fees. During this period I spent periods of time working in other sections in order to broaden my experience and ability, these included Internal Audit, Education Accountancy, and Cashiers.

On qualification as an accounting technician, I was appointed as the assistant to the Section Head of the Social Services Accountancy Section. The Section Head is a qualified member of the Chartered Institute of Public Finance and Accountancy (CIPFA). The majority of accountants employed in local government and the Health Service are members of this professional accounting body.

My duties involve the preparation and provision of accounting information for the services provided by the Social Services Committee, and I also complete special assignments which are allocated to me by the Section Head.

I am responsible for the preparation of the budget for the Social Services Committee under the supervision of the Section Head. I prepare estimates of the level of expenditure for the next financial year based on guidance issued by the Council Social Services Committee and the Treasurer relating to the funds available from government grants, rates, and income from charges for services. I compile the budget based on these estimates and it is submitted to the Social Services Committee and Council for approval.

The budgetary control system is computer-based. As expenditure is incurred, items such as salaries and wages are coded to budget heads. Weekly tabulations are produced in the computer section which is located in the Treasurer's Department; these show the actual and budgeted expenditure for each budget head, and any variances are highlighted.

I have to ensure that these tabulations are accurate and I prepare a summary for the Section Head. I also send out budgetary control statements to the various social services establishments on a monthly basis. If a particular budget head is overspent, I will request an explanation from the person responsible within the establishment, together with their proposals on how to remedy the situation. I have to report any problems to the Section Head.

My other main responsibility is the production of the annual **Revenue Account** and Balance Sheet for the Social Services Committee. The Revenue Account is equivalent to the Trading and Profit and Loss Account in the private sector. This involves closing down the accounts on 31st March each year and calculating the amounts of debtors and creditors as well as obtaining stock values from managers in the various Social Services establishments. The accounts I prepare are checked by the Section Head and Chief Accountant and are then subject to an external audit by an external auditor appointed by the **Audit Commission** who has to certify that all the accounts prepared by the various services properly present the financial affairs of the County Council. As you can imagine, I have to answer all questions and queries the external auditor may have on the Social Services Accounts.

Some of the special tasks I have completed recently include a review of the budgetary control system with the Section Head and a review of energy costs and control in our residential old persons home in conjunction with our Internal Audit Section.

Some members of our Association go on to study for the CIPFA Professional Examinations. To do this you need to have reached a particular standard in the Association's qualifying examinations.

Accounting Technicians are not only employed in local government; the number employed in the health service, industry, and private practice is increasing all the time as managers become aware of the value of the role fulfilled by accounting technicians.

Activity 3

Go to your college or public library and list all the Accountancy journals available there. Find the sections in the journals where vacancies are advertised for accountancy personnel:

1 What professional accountancy qualifications are applicants required to possess for accountant posts advertised in the following types of organization?
   a retailing
   b manufacturing
   c banking or insurance

2 What additional benefits are offered for vacancies advertised for a
   a Chartered Accountant
   b Management Accountant
   c Public Finance Accountant?

3 What is the meaning of the following designatory letters used by qualified accountants?
   a ACA
   b FCMA
   c FCCA
   d AAT
   e FCA

4 Not all advertisements give details of the salary offered, but for those advertisements which do disclose salary levels find the vacancy offering the highest salary. Are the reasons for such a high salary disclosed in the advertisement?

Summary

This block introduced you to the various people who either prepare or use accounting information. The people interviewed are all involved in the different aspects of accounting, either recording financial transactions or summarizing accounting information for the owners or managers of a business.

The block that follows details how the financial transactions of a business are recorded using the double entry book-keeping system. It is necessary for the accounting records of a business to be maintained both consistently and accurately as they are the source for the production of accounting information, used to measure and monitor the performance of a business.

Block 3
Accounting Systems and Records

Introduction

The previous block introduced you to the various people involved in accounting, in particular you were introduced to the proprietor of The Golf Shop, a Mr. S. Wing. You should also now be aware that the production of accounting information is based on the accounting records that are maintained within a business to record all the financial transactions that take place.

This block details the accounting procedures involved in the maintenance of accounting records and details some of the main concepts and conventions of accounting involved in this process. The examples used throughout this block relate to the small business owned and run by S. Wing.

Book-keeping

In order to keep account of money spent and received, a business needs to keep a record of its financial transactions. The owner or owners of a business and other individuals and institutions such as banks are all interested in the **performance** of a business over a period of time and also in the **financial** position of a business at a particular point in time.

There is therefore a need for the **accurate recording** of the various financial transactions of a business, and the process of recording these transactions is known as **book-keeping**. The previous block contained an interview with a book-keeper in a public limited company. As this interview described, the process of book-keeping has changed over recent years, and there are various book-keeping packages available for use on micro-computers which make the process of book-keeping more efficient. In particular the volume of work performed by a book-keeper is greatly reduced.

The traditional system of book-keeping is known as the **double-entry system**. The basic rule is that every transaction is entered in the **ledger** twice.

Ledger Entries

A ledger is a bound book, or series of books, in which the various accounts which record the financial transactions of a business are maintained. Depending on the size of a business, the ledger may contain hundreds or even thousands of individual accounts, and is usually divided into sections, each containing a separate **classification** of account. The diagram below illustrates how a ledger is divided and the accounts classified:

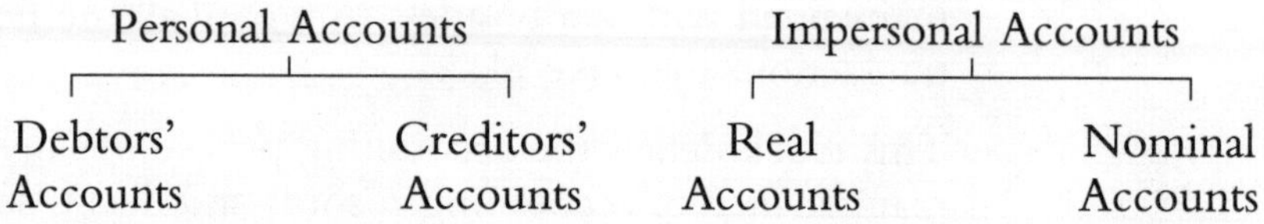

Personal Accounts		Impersonal Accounts	
Debtors' Accounts	Creditors' Accounts	Real Accounts	Nominal Accounts

Debtors' accounts are opened for each individual or business organization to which goods or services are sold on credit. **Debtors** are therefore individuals or organizations who owe a business money.

Creditors' accounts are opened for each individual or business organization from which goods or services are purchased on credit. Creditors are therefore individuals or organizations who are owed money by a business.

Real accounts are maintained for each **asset** owned by a business. A **fixed asset** is an item which will remain the property of the business for more than one financial year. Examples of fixed assets include land, buildings, machinery, and vehicles. A **current asset** is an item which will be used or consumed in the course of trading in a financial year. Examples of current assets include stocks of raw materials and stocks of finished goods for resale.

Nominal accounts are maintained to record sales and purchases, and the **expenses** incurred by the business such as electricity, rates, and the payment of wages.

The cost of buying a fixed asset is termed **capital expenditure**, whereas the cost of buying stocks of raw materials or paying expenses such as rates is termed **revenue expenditure**.

Activity 1

Classify the following accounts under the headings Personal, Real, or Nominal.

a Sales Account
b Electricity Account
c Rent Account
d Vehicles Account
e J. Blackburn Account
f Stationery Account

Activity 2

Classify the following business transactions of The Golf Shop which is owned and run by S. Wing under the headings of **capital expenditure** and **revenue expenditure**.

a Purchase of stock of golfing sweaters for £2,000
b Purchase of a van for business use for £5,000
c Payment of an electricity bill for £480
d Purchase of an receipting machine for £500
e Repairs to shop front door costing £100
f Payments of £350 to a builder for constructing a sports training shoe display rack.

The pages of a ledger are laid out as follows:

Date	Particulars	Folio	£	p	Date	Particulars	Folio	£	p

The Cash Account is further divided into two columns to separate transactions involving the receipt or payment of cash and the payment for goods or services by cheque.

Date	Particulars	Folio	Cash		Bank		Date	Particulars	Folio	Cash		Bank	
			£	p	£	p				£	p	£	p

The left hand side of the ledger shown on page 33 is called the **debit side** and the right hand side is called the **credit side**. This rule applies throughout the ledger regardless of the classification of the account.

Each time a financial transaction occurs it is recorded in two accounts in the ledger. This is known as the **duality concept**, ie for every **debit** entry made there is a **credit** entry.

A **debit** entry, an entry on the left hand side of the page represents an **inflow** into the business.

A **credit** entry, an entry on the right hand side of the page represents an **outflow** from the business.

The diagram opposite illustrates the **duality concept** and the process of recording transactions on the **debit side** and **credit side** of the various ledger accounts.

To summarize the process:
A debit entry represents an asset or a receipt in the form of cash or services/expenses received or consumed by the business. A credit entry represents a liability or a payment.

For each transaction the date, details, and amount are recorded. As each account in the ledger may appear on a separate page, the recording of the page or **folio number** allows easy cross-referencing or tracing of transactions. For example the cash account may be on page 2 of the ledger and the cash sales account on page 16. When a cash sale is made and a debit entry recorded in the Cash Account, a figure 16 will be written in the folio column.

In the illustrations and activities that follow, a simplified format of ledger accounts is used. This is the traditional 'T' account layout with the folio column excluded.

A Worked Example

To illustrate the double entry book-keeping system we will use the example of S. Wing, who opens a shop selling golfing and other sports equipment. We will look at his first month of trading and record the transactions in the appropriate ledger accounts.

1 S. Wing commenced trading on 1st January 19X1. He transferred £25,000 from his private bank account to a business bank account he had opened at a local bank.

Debit Entry **Credit Entry**

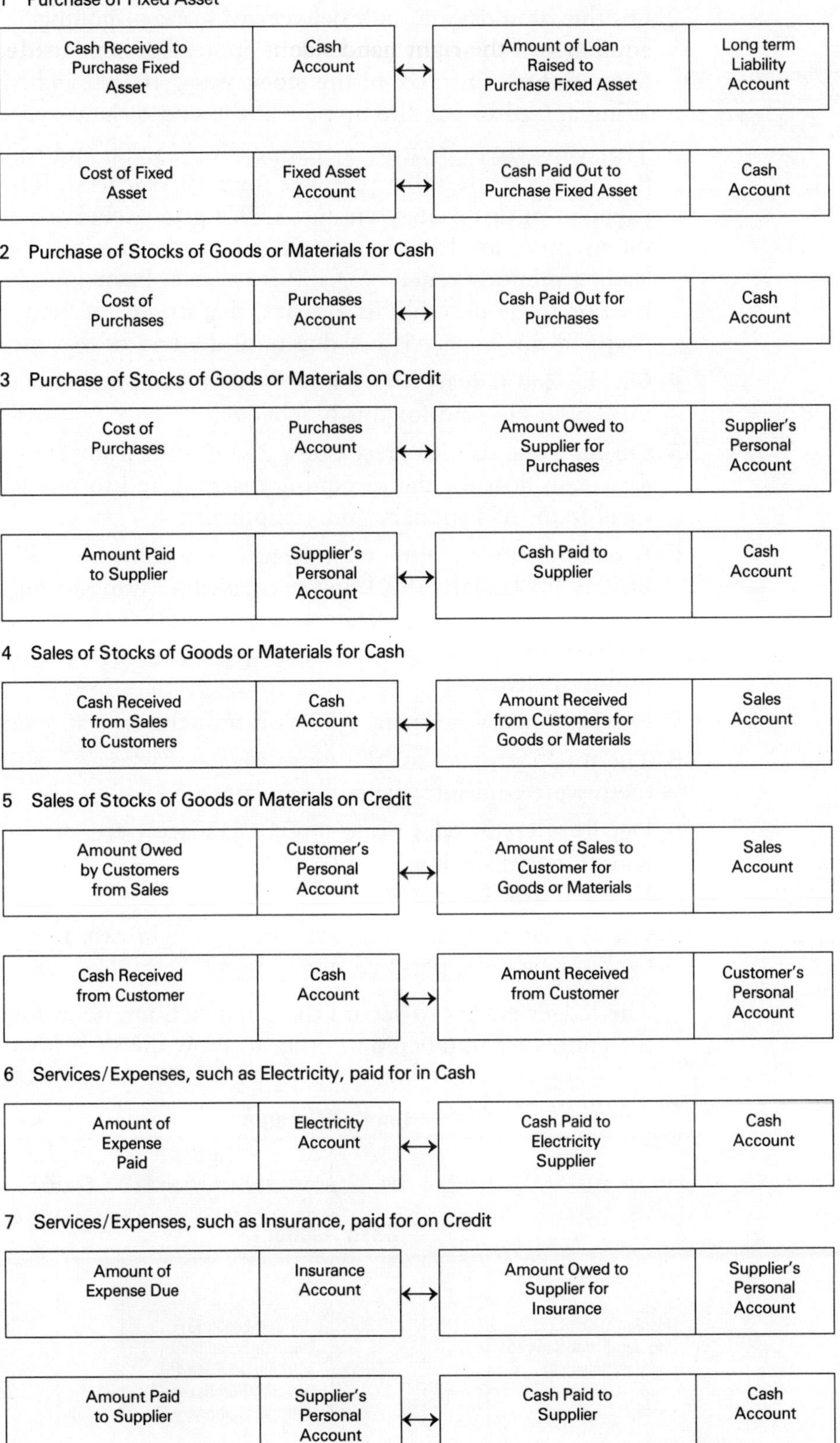

2 On the same day he took delivery of stock of golfing equipment and sports goods from Sports Equipment Supplies Ltd. The cost of this stock was £10,000 and Mr Wing agreed to pay the invoice at the end of January.

3 That same day, he wrote a cheque for £15,000 and paid the owners of the shop premises for a 15 year lease. The payment of this money entitles S. Wing to exclusive use of the premises for 15 years. In addition to the purchase of the lease, a monthly rental of £400 is payable. Payment of rent is to be made monthly **in arrears**, that means the rent payment for January is not due until the end of that month.

4 On the 2nd January 19X1 he bought a receipting machine for £500. He paid for this by cheque.

5 On the same day he drew out £250 in cash from the bank for a cash float for the receipting machine and to purchase small items of stationery and equipment.

6 A representative from a manufacturing organization called on the 3rd January 19X1 and persuaded S. Wing to buy some stock of golfing sweaters costing £2,000. As this was a special offer, S. Wing wrote a cheque for £2,000 to ensure prompt delivery.

7 On 5th January he spent £50 cash on items of stationery.

8 The total cash sales for the month January were £7,000, these were paid into the bank account.

9 Details of credit sales made on 31st January were:
King Edward's School £200
Vale Football Club £700

10 On 31st January, S. Wing drew out £500 in cash from the bank for his own personal use.

The ledger entries to record these transactions are as follows, the entries are numbered in order to show the steps involved.

Capital Account

	£		£
		1st Jan Bank Account (1)	£25,000

Cash Account

	Cash £	Bank £		Cash £	Bank £
1st Jan Capital (1)		25,000	1st Jan Lease (3)		15,000
2nd Jan From Bank (5)	250		2nd Jan Equipment (4)		500
31st Jan Sales (8)		7,000	2nd Jan To Cash (5)		250
			3rd Jan Purchases (6)		2,000
			5th Jan Stationery (7)	50	

Cash Account

	Cash £	Bank £		Cash £	Bank £
			31st Jan Drawings (10)		500
			31st Jan Balance c/d		13,750
		£32,000			£32,000
31st Jan Bal b/d		£13,750			

Purchases Account

	£		£
1st Jan Sports Equip. Supplies Ltd. (2)	10,000		
3rd Jan Cash (6)	2,000		

Sports Equipment Supplies Ltd. Account

	£		£
		Jan Purchases (2)	10,000

Shop Lease Account

	£		£
1st Jan Cash (3)	15,000		

Fixtures and Fittings Account

	£		£
2nd Jan Cash (4)	500		

Stationery Account

	£		£
5th Jan Cash (7)	50		

Sales Account

	£		£
		1st Jan Cash (8)	7,000
		31st Jan King Edward's School (9)	200
		31st Jan Vale Football Club (9)	700

King Edward's School Account

	£		£
31st Jan Sales (9)	200		

Vale Football Club Account

	£		£
31st Jan Sales (9)	700		

S. Wing Drawings Account

	£		£
31st Jan cash (10)	500		

The next operation in recording the financial transactions of S. Wing for the month of January is to **balance off** or **rule off** the accounts at the end of January. If we look at the bank column in the Cash Account the operation is completed as follows:

Step	Operation
1	Add up the debit and credit sides. Which side is the greater?
2	Since the debit side (£32,000) is greater than the credit side (£18,250), we know that the balancing figure must be £13,750 (£32,000 – £18,250). This is the amount of cash S. Wing has in the bank at the end of the month.
3	Enter the balance on the **light** side, that is the side with the smallest total. In the credit side of the bank column we therefore enter £13,750.
4	Rule off the account with a space for the total, the totals should be entered on the same line on both sides of the account. Double underline the totals. In the bank column the total is £32,000.
5	Carry down the balance already calculated to the opposite side. In the bank column this is £13,750.
6	The balance brought down represents the cash at the bank as at midnight on 31st January 19X1. This of course is also the starting balance on 1st February 19X1.

Activity 3

Balance off the Cash column in the Cash Account and the other accounts for S. Wing as at 31st January 19X1.

The balances brought down you should have calculated are as follows:

Account	Debit £	Credit £
Capital		25,000
Cash – Cash column	200	
– Bank column	13,750	
Purchases	12,000	
Sports Equipment Supplies Ltd.		10,000
Shop Lease	15,000	
Fixtures and Fittings	500	
Stationery	50	
Sales		7,900
King Edward's School	200	
Vale Football Club	700	
S. Wing—Drawings	500	

You will have noticed that a separate account was opened to record the drawing of £500 cash from the business for S. Wing's personal use. From the interviews with the various people involved in accounting we have become aware that one of the purposes of maintaining financial records is to measure how successful a business is in terms of making a **profit and loss** on its trading activities. Records of business financial transactions are kept separate from personal financial transactions. This is known as the **entity** concept: the business is treated as a separate individual.

Another important area for discussion is the distinction between the recording of the purchase of the receipting machine for the shop, and the purchase of stationery. The purchase of the receipting machine is obviously treated as capital expenditure, as it will be used in the business for a period of more than one financial year. The purchase of stationery for £50 included a stapler for £6 and a small electronic calculator for £5. Although in theory these purchases could be treated as capital expenditure, as they will be used in the business for a period of more than one financial year, items of this type are treated as an **expense**. This is because the concept of **materiality** states that only items whose cost is significant in relation to the overall value of the business should be treated as capital expenditure and recorded as a **fixed asset**.

Activity 4

Record the following transactions for February 19X1 in the ledger accounts of S. Wing. Do not forget you will need to record in each account the balances brought down on 1st February 19X1 (these were calculated in Activity 3) and balance off the accounts as at 28th February 19X1.

1 1st February
Stock was delivered costing £8,000 from Sports Equipment Supplies Ltd. S. Wing agreed to pay the invoice for these goods at the end of February.

2 2nd February
S. Wing sent a cheque for £590 to the Mindatrest Insurance Company. The insurance policy covers fires, public liability, and accidental damage to his stock and shop fixtures and fittings.

3 3rd February
A cheque for £200 was received and banked from King Edward's school for sports equipment supplied in January.

4 4th February
A cheque for £10,000 was sent to Sports Equipment Supplies Ltd.

5 5th February
A contractor completes work on the installation of a burglar alarm system for the shop. The cost of this work was £600 and S. Wing paid the contractor by cheque.

6 12th February
The treasurer of Vale Football Club called at the shop and gave S. Wing a cheque for £500 in part settlement of the amount owed for football kit and footballs supplied to them in January. S. Wing banked the cheque.

7 20th February
Stock of golf clubs costing £6,500 were delivered from Ting Clubs Ltd. S. Wing agreed to pay for these at the end of March.

8 24th February
A cheque for £300 was sent to the local authority for rates due from 1st January to 31st March 19X1.

9 25th February
S. Wing spent £20 on stationery.

10 26th February
S. Wing purchased a display unit for £100 cash.

11 27th February
A delivery of golfing shoes costing £2,000 was received. S. Wing wrote a cheque and gave it to the delivery van driver.

12 28th February
S. Wing drew out £600 in cash from the bank for his own personal use.

13 The total cash sales for the month of February was £11,000; these were paid into the bank account.

The Trial Balance

A trial balance is a list of the accounts in the ledger with the amounts of their balances brought down. The **duality** concept implies that there should be a credit entry for every debit entry. When accounts are balanced off the debit balances brought down should therefore equal the credit balances brought down.

As its name implies, the trial balance is in fact a 'trial' to check the accuracy of the book-keeping entries, and to bring to light such things as errors in the addition of the columns of figures in the accounts, the omission of one of the double entries, or the recording of a transaction in the ledger account twice on the same side.

Activity 5

The trial balance will not disclose all the possible book-keeping errors that can occur. Discuss in groups what errors you think will not be disclosed by a trial balance.

The following errors are not disclosed by a trial balance:

1 Error of omission
2 Error of commission
3 Error of original entry
4 Error of duplication
5 Error of principle
6 Compensating errors

A trial balance can be produced at any time. Look again at Activity 3, and the list of debit and credit balances on page 38. If you add up all the balances in the Debit column, you will see that they equal the total of the balances in Credit column; this total is £42,900. The list of balances brought down on page 38 is of course the Trial Balance for S. Wing as at 31st January 19X1.

Activity 6

Produce a Trial Balance for S. Wing as at 28th February 19X1 using the balances brought down in the accounts that you calculated in Activity 4.

No transactions occurred in February 19X1 which affected the shop lease account. The treatment of this account at the end of February 19X1 is shown below. You will need to include the balance brought down on 1st March 19X1 on this account in your trial balance.

Shop Lease Account

	£		£
1st Feb balance b/d	15,000	28th Feb balance c/d	15,000
	£15,000		£15,000
1st March balance b/d	15,000		

The totals of the Trial balance are £58,400

A trial balance is normally produced at the end of a **financial year** as the performance of a business is measured in relation to a particular financial year. At the end of a financial year the accounts of a business are balanced off and a trial balance is produced.

S. Wing commenced business on 1st January 19X1, so the financial year in relation to his business runs from 1st January 19X1 to midnight on the 31st December 19X1. If S. Wing had started trading on the 1st February 19X1 the financial year would be:

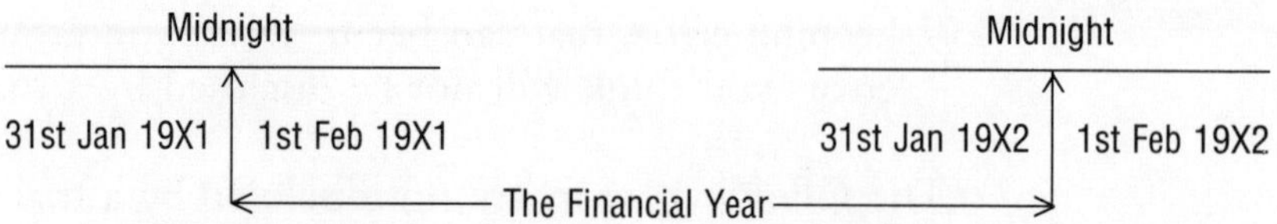

S. Wing's financial year would end on 31st Jan 19X2, and all the accounts would be balanced off as at 31st January 19X2.

The date on which the financial year of business ends is therefore related to the date on which that business was commenced and can therefore be at any time. However the financial year in public sector organizations such as local authorities runs from 1st April to 31st March, this is in line with the Central Government accounting system and is a statutory requirement.

Activity 7

S. Wing balances off the accounts in his ledger on 31st December 19X1 and draws up the following trial balance:

Account	Debit £	Credit £
Capital		25,000
Cash at bank	5,000	
Cash in hand	345	
Purchases	96,000	
Sports Equipment Supplies		3,200
Shop lease	15,000	
Fixtures and Fittings	2,500	
Stationery	205	
Sales		114,800
Vale Football Club	200	
Drawings	8,800	
Rates	1,500	
Insurance	290	
Electricity	1,200	
Telephone	600	
Advertising	1,050	
Vehicle	5,000	
Rent	4,000	
Vehicle running expenses	790	
	£142,480	£143,000

To his dismay he finds the trial balance does not balance! He spends many hours looking through all the invoices, receipts, cheque books, and bank statements relating to his business trying to find any items he has forgotten to enter in the ledger. He also checks all the additions and balances carried down in the ledger accounts for any mistakes.

The following is a list of what he found:

1 The rent payment of £400 for November had been completely omitted from the accounts. S. Wing had drawn a cheque on 6th December 19X1.

2 Credit Sales of £600 to The Castle Golf Club have been included in the sales account but no personal account has been opened to record the money owed by the Golf Club.

3 The purchase of a fire extinguisher for the shop has been recorded in the Fixtures and Fittings account. The payment of £90 cash has not been recorded in the cash account.

4 The vehicle running expenses account was undercast by £10.

Redraft the trial balance drawn up by S. Wing to take account of the errors listed above.

Control Accounts

S. Wing's accounts are all kept in one ledger and, as we have seen, a trial balance is extracted to test the arithmetical accuracy of the ledger accounts. We must also remember that certain errors are not revealed by a trial balance.

If the trial balance totals disagree, it is quite a straightforward exercise in a small business to check all the accounting entries to locate the errors. However, as a business grows, the number of transactions will increase and there may be many thousands of sales and purchases ledger account entries.

It is usual, therefore, as a business grows, to maintain separate Sales and Purchases Ledgers in addition to the General Ledger. This process was described by the book-keeper in a public limited company in Block 2.

Control or **Total Accounts** are maintained to check the arithmetical accuracy of each ledger. Control Accounts perform the same function as a trial balance for a particular ledger and **do not** form part of the double-entry book-keeping system. **Total** figures are used in Control Accounts as an **arithmetic proof** of the various balances in the personal accounts in the Sales and Purchases Ledgers. The format is as follows:

Sales Ledger Control Account

	£		£
Total Balances b/d	X	Total Cash from Sales	X
Total Sales	X	Total Sales Returns	X
		Total Balances c/d	X
Total Balances b/d	XX		XX

Purchase Ledger Control Account

	£		£
Total Cash Paid	X	Total Balances b/d	X
Total Purchases Returns	X	Total Purchases	X
Total Balances c/d	X		
	XX		XX
		Total Balances b/d	X

These are also known as the Total Debtors Control Account and Total Creditors Control Account.

Computer Based Accounting

There are various accounting packages available for micro-computers and these are now widely used in all types and size of business organization.

Various software manufacturers market these accounting packages and they vary in sophistication. Most packages available have a variety of versions or systems and the user will need to select the appropriate system which will cater for the volume of accounting transactions that will need to be recorded and the financial reports required to measure the performance of the business.

An accounting package therefore contains a "hierarchy of systems", a typical hierarchy is as follows:

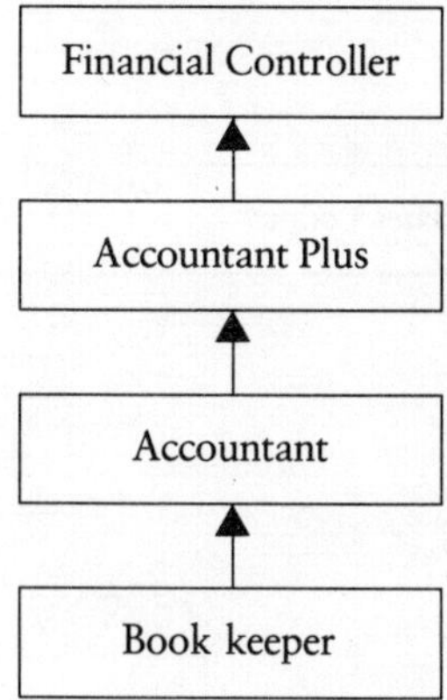

The Book-keeper System will provide three main ledgers in which the accounting transactions of a business can be recorded. This type of system is suitable for a small business where the number of Sales, Purchase, and Nominal Accounts do not exceed 1,000. This system will also produce a trial balance and profit and loss account.

The facilities and capabilities increase depending on the package purchased. The Financial Controller System, the most sophisticated, offers all the features contained in the other packages, such as the production of a trial balance, Profit and Loss Account, and Balance Sheet, but will also give a detailed analysis of business performance stock control information.

Activity 8

List all the advantages and disadvantages to a small business such as S. Wing's of purchasing a micro-computer and an Accounting Package.

What type of system would you recommend to S. Wing?

It is very likely that a small businessman like S. Wing would purchase a micro-computer and an accounting package as soon as the funds are available. In Activity 4 you will have discussed the advantages and disadvantages of such a purchase. The main advantages you should have identified are speed, accuracy, and reliability of information. The main disadvantages are the time required to learn how to operate the package, and of course the cost of the micro-computer.

A typical system is arranged as follows:

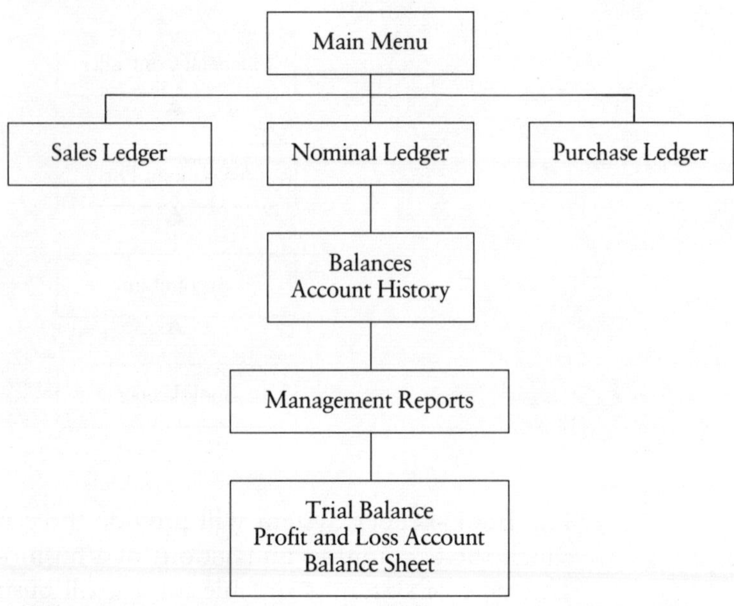

The main menu contains all the **options** available in the system, typical options include **initialization, Sales Ledger posting** and **management reports.**

When the system is purchased the first stage is to 'initialize' the accounts which will be maintained with the three ledgers. The various accounts are named and coded depending on the type of transaction that will be recorded in them. The coding system varies depending on the package purchased, but a typical coding system is based on a four-digit system as follows:

Code	Type of Account
0000 ⟶	Fixed Asset Accounts
0035 ⟶	Accounts to record current Assets and Liabilities
0090 ⟶	Capital Accounts
1000 ⟶	Trading Accounts (Sales)
2000 ⟶	Trading Accounts (Purchases)
2500 ⟶	Trading Accounts (Expenses)

When the accounts have been set up, the transactions are posted to the accounts by selecting the Sales Ledger Posting option. A 'posting screen' or 'posting window', similar to the one shown at the top of the next page, for posting Sales Invoices to the Sales Ledger Accounts, will be displayed.

Sales Invoices ☐ Accountant Plus ☐ Date:

Account Name

Account Code

Account Number ☐ Date ☐ Invoice Details Amount ☐ VAT ☐ Total

The transactions are entered in the shaded grid.

If the Management Reports option is selected, a variety of secondary options or Management Report options are offered. These include a monthly Accounts option which gives the user of the package the ability to produce a Profit and Loss Account and Balance Sheet for the current month and to date. These are referred to in later blocks.

Using the Report facility enables the user to close off the various ledger accounts at the month end. If a typical book-keeping system had been used to record the accounting transactions of S. Wing in his first month of trading which ended on 31st January, 19X1, the computer print-out produced would be in the following format. Please note the computer print-out shows 31st January, 19X1 as 310191.

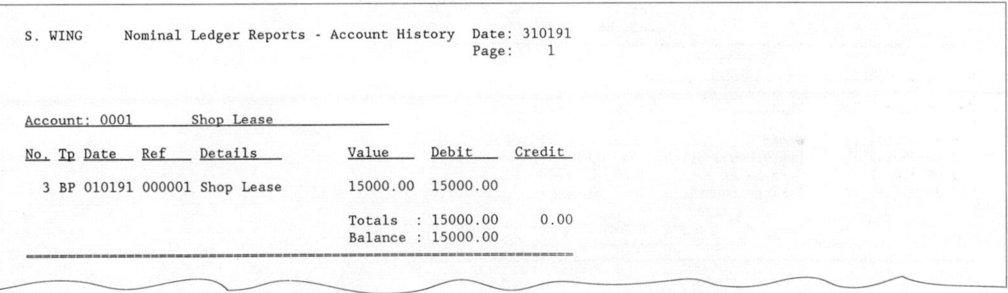

```
S. WING     Nominal Ledger Reports - Account History  Date: 310191
                                                      Page:     1

Account: 0001       Shop Lease

No. Tp Date   Ref    Details          Value     Debit     Credit

  3 BP 010191 000001 Shop Lease       15000.00  15000.00

                                      Totals  : 15000.00      0.00
                                      Balance : 15000.00
```

Account: 0005 Fixtures & Fittings

No.	Tp	Date	Ref	Details	Value	Debit	Credit
4	BP	020191	000002	Receipting Machine	500.00	500.00	
					Totals :	500.00	0.00
					Balance :	500.00	

Account: 0090 Capital Invested - S. Wing

No.	Tp	Date	Ref	Details	Value	Debit	Credit
1	BR	010191		Capital Invested	25000.00		25000.00
					Totals :	0.00	25000.00
					Balance :		25000.00

Account: 0091 Drawings - S. Wing

No.	Tp	Date	Ref	Details	Value	Debit	Credit
14	BP	310191	000005	Drawings	500.00	500.00	
					Totals :	500.00	0.00
					Balance :	500.00	

Account: 10001 Sales

No.	Tp	Date	Ref	Details	Value	Debit	Credit
9	CR	310191		Cash sales	7000.00		7000.00
12	SI	310191	s0001	Sports Equipment	200.00		200.00
13	SI	310191	s0002	Sports Equipment	700.00		700.00
					Totals :	0.00	7900.00
					Balance :		7900.00

Account: 2001 Purchases

No.	Tp	Date	Ref	Details	Value	Debit	Credit
2	PI	010191	p0001	Sports Equipment	10000.00	10000.00	
7	BP	030191	000004	Golfing Sweaters	2000.00	2000.00	
					Totals :	12000.00	0.00
					Balance :	12000.00	

Account: 3004 Stationery

No.	Tp	Date	Ref	Details	Value	Debit	Credit
8	CP	050191		Letterheads etc	50.00	50.00	
					Totals :	50.00	0.00
					Balance :	50.00	

Account: 0089 Bank

No.	Tp	Date	Ref	Details	Value	Debit	Credit
1	BR	010191		Capital Invested	25000.00	25000.00	
3	BP	010191	000001	Shop Lease	15000.00		15000.00
4	BP	020191	000002	Receipting Machine	500.00		500.00
6	JC	020191	j1	000003	250.00		250.00
7	BP	030191	000004	Golfing Sweaters	2000.00		2000.00
11	JD	310191	j2	Takings Banked	7000.00	7000.00	
14	BP	310191	000005	Drawings	500.00		500.00
					Totals :	32000.00	18250.00
					Balance :	13750.00	

Account: 0088 Cash

No.	Tp	Date	Ref	Details	Value	Debit	Credit
5	JD	020191	j1	Float	250.00	250.00	
8	CP	050191		Letterheads etc	50.00		50.00
9	CR	310191		Cash Sales	7000.00	7000.00	
10	JC	310191	j2	Takings Banked	7000.00		7000.00
					Totals :	7250.00	7050.00
					Balance :	200.00	

S. WING Purchase Ledger Reports - Account History Date: 310191
Page: 1

Account: SESL Sports Equ. Supplies Ltd.

No.	Tp	Date	Ref	Details	Value	Debit	Credit
2	PI	010191	p0001	Sports Equipment	10000.00		10000.00

Amount outstanding : 10000.00
Amount paid this period : 0.00
Credit limit : 0.00

S. WING Purchase Ledger Reports - Account Balances Date: 310191
Page: 1

A/C	Account Name	Turnover	Credit Limit	Balance	Current	30 days	60 days	90 days	Older
SESL	Sports Equ. Supplies Ltd.	10000.00	0.00	10000.00	0.00	10000.00	0.00	0.00	0.00
	Totals :	10000.00	0.00	10000.00	0.00	10000.00	0.00	0.00	0.00

S. WING Sales Ledger Reports - Account History Date: 310191
Page: 1

Account: KES King Edward School

No.	Tp	Date	Ref	Details	Value	Debit	Credit
12	SI	310191	s0001	Sports Equipment	200.00	200.00	

Amount outstanding : 200.00
Amount paid this period : 0.00
Credit limit : 0.00

Account: VFC Vale Football Club

No.	Tp	Date	Ref	Details	Value	Debit	Credit
13	SI	310191	s0002	Sports Equipment	700.00	700.00	

Amount outstanding : 700.00
Amount paid this period : 0.00
Credit limit : 0.00

S. WING Sales Ledger Reports - Account Balances Date: 310191
Page: 1

A/C	Account Name	Turnover	Credit Limit	Balance	Current	30 days	60 days	90 days	Older
KES	King Edward School	200.00	0.00	200.00	200.00	0.00	0.00	0.00	0.00
VFC	Vale Football Club	700.00	0.00	700.00	700.00	0.00	0.00	0.00	0.00
	Totals :	900.00	0.00	900.00	900.00	0.00	0.00	0.00	0.00

S. WING Control Accounts - Creditor's Control Date: 310191
Page: 1

Account: 0065 Creditor's Control

No.	Tp	Date	Ref	Details	Value	Debit	Credit
2	PI	010191	p0001	Sports Equipment	10000.00		10000.00
					Totals :	0.00	10000.00
					Balance :		10000.00

S. WING Control Accounts - Debtor's Control Date: 310191
Page: 1

Account: 0038 Debtor's Control

No.	Tp	Date	Ref	Details	Value	Debit	Credit
12	SI	310191	s0001	Sports Equipment	200.00	200.00	
13	SI	310191	s0002	Sports Equipment	700.00	700.00	
					Totals :	900.00	0.00
					Balance :	900.00	

S. WING Management Reports - Audit Trail Date: 310191
Page: 1

No.	Type	A/C	N/C	Dep	Details	Date	Inv	Net Amount	Tax Amount	TC	Paid	Date	Cheque	Amount Paid	N-AC	N-NC
1	BR		0090	0	Capital Invested	010191		25000.00	0.00	TO	Y	010191		25000.00	0	0
2	PI	SESL	2001	0	Sports Equipment	010191	p0001	10000.00	0.00	TO	N			0.00	0	7
3	BP		0001	0	Shop Lease	010191	000001	15000.00	0.00	TO	Y	010191	000001	15000.00	0	0
4	BP		0005	0	Receipting Machine	020191	000002	500.00	0.00	TO	Y	020191	000002	500.00	0	0
5	JD		0088	0	Float	020191	j1	250.00	0.00	TO	Y	020191	j1	250.00	0	10
6	JC		0089	0	000003	020191	j1	250.00	0.00	TO	Y	020191	j1	250.00	0	11
7	BP		2001	0	Golfing Sweaters	030191	000004	2000.00	0.00	TO	Y	030191	000004	2000.00	0	0
8	CP		3004	0	Letterheads etc	050191		50.00	0.00	TO	Y	050191		50.00	0	0
9	CR		1001	0	Cash Sales	310191		7000.00	0.00	TO	Y	310191		7000.00	0	12
10	JC		0088	0	Takings Banked	310191	j2	7000.00	0.00	TO	Y	310191	j2	7000.00	0	0
11	JD		0089	0	Takings Banked	310191	j2	7000.00	0.00	TO	Y	310191	j2	7000.00	0	0
12	SI	KES	1001	0	Sports Equipment	310191	s0001	200.00	0.00	TO	N			0.00	0	13
13	SI	VFC	1001	0	Sports Equipment	310191	s0002	700.00	0.00	TO	N			0.00	0	0
14	BP		0091	0	Drawings	310191	000005	500.00	0.00	TO	Y	310191	000005	500.00	0	0

S. WING Nominal Ledger Reports - Trial Balance Date: 310191
Page: 1

Ref	Account Name	Debit	Credit
0001	Shop Lease	15000.00	
0005	Fixtures & Fittings	500.00	
0038	Debtor's Control	900.00	
0065	Creditor's Control		10000.00
0088	Cash	200.00	
0089	Bank	13750.00	
0090	Capital Invested - S. Wing		25000.00
0091	Drawings - S. Wing	500.00	
1001	Sales		7900.00
2001	Purchases	12000.00	
3004	Stationery	50.00	
		42900.00	42900.00

As you can see the system will produce appropriate Control Accounts and a Trial Balance as at the end of January 19X1. An Audit Trial is also produced which numbers every transaction from 1st January to 31st January.

Activity 9

Either Find out if an accounting package is available for use on the micro-computers in your college. If so, obtain the manual relating to the package and list the facilities available.

Or Look through the Accounting journals in your college library and list all the packages that are advertised. How do they vary and what hierarchy of systems is available for each package advertised?

Summary

Accounting is concerned with **measurement**, and book-keeping provides the basis for the information on which the owners of a business can measure in money terms the **performance** of that business. At the end of a **financial year** the owner or owners of a business will want a measure of the **worth** of the business; how much it owes, how much it is owed, for instance. The owners will also wish to know if they earned a **profit** or **loss** during a financial year.

Block 4
Trading and Profit and Loss Accounts

Introduction

This block will look at how the financial performance of a business is measured by the production of a Trading Account and a Profit and Loss Account. In particular we will look at S. Wing's business accounts at the end of his first year of trading.

The various accounts maintained in the ledger form the basis for the preparation of the Trading and Profit and Loss Accounts. Before these can be prepared we must consider some of the adjustments and provisions that have to be taken into account in line with the various concepts and conventions of accounting. Some of these concepts and conventions were discussed in the previous block. This block will introduce you to others relating to the adjustments and provisions described.

The Trading Account

The Trading Account is the ledger account in which the Gross Profit earned by a business is calculated for a financial year. Gross profit can be expressed as follows:

Gross Profit	=	Sales – Cost of Sales
Cost of Sales	=	Cost of Goods sold
Cost of Goods Sold	=	Opening Stock + Purchases – Closing Stock

The Trading Account is part of the double entry book-keeping system and the format is as follows:

Trading Account

	£		£
Opening Stock	X	Sales	X
Purchases	X	Closing Stock	X
Gross Profit*	X		
	£XX		£XX

* This is the balancing figure on the account: the opposite credit entry is made on the credit side of the Profit and Loss Account.

The Problem of Stock

At the end of a financial year, a business which manufactures a product or buys stocks of goods or materials for resale will have a stock of raw materials, finished goods, or goods or materials for resale. In the case of S. Wing this will be stock of golf clubs, sweaters, and other sports equipment he has in his shop and stockroom at midnight on 31st December each year, i.e. the end of each financial year.

In order to calculate the cost of the stock held by a business at the end of a financial year, all the items in stock have to be counted and their value calculated based on the **price paid** for various items in stock. This process is known as **stocktaking**.

At the end of S. Wing's first year of trading, all the items of stock in his shop and small storeroom at the rear are counted and listed on **stocktaking sheets**. The cost of the various items are ascertained from invoices from suppliers, and the total cost of all items held in stock is calculated. For the financial year ended 31st December 19X1 this was £15,000.

A stock account is opened in the ledger and the following entries are made:

Stock Account

	£		£
31st December 19X1 Trading A/C	15,000		

Trading Account

	£		£
		31st December 19X1 Closing Stock	15,000

At the end of S. Wing's second year of trading, 31st December 19X2, the closing stock is £22,000. These entries are made:

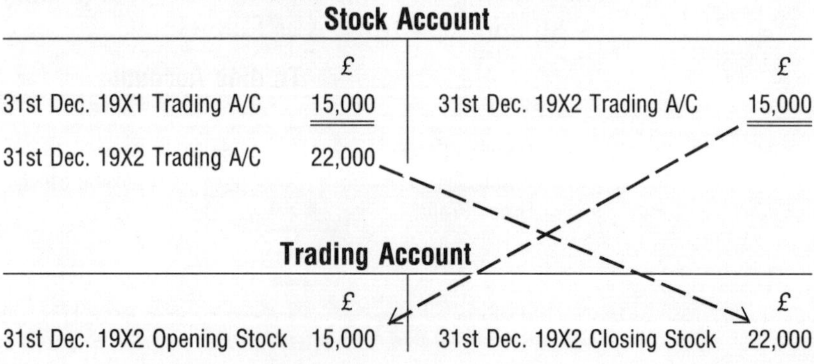

Stock Account

	£		£
31st Dec. 19X1 Trading A/C	15,000	31st Dec. 19X2 Trading A/C	15,000
31st Dec. 19X2 Trading A/C	22,000		

Trading Account

	£		£
31st Dec. 19X2 Opening Stock	15,000	31st Dec. 19X2 Closing Stock	22,000

The balance on the stock account, a debit balance, is carried forward into the next accounting period. Stock is a **current asset** and appears in the Balance Sheet under that heading.

The Profit and Loss Account

The Profit and Loss Account is the ledger account in which the **net profit earned** or the **net loss incurred** by a business is calculated for a financial year.

net profit = gross profit – expenses

If the **expenses** consumed are greater than the **gross profit earned** then the business will have **incurred a net loss**.

The Profit and Loss Account is part of the double-entry book-keeping system and the format is as follows:

Profit and Loss Account

	£		£
Expenses	X	Gross Profit (Note 1)	X
Net Profit (Note 2)	X		

Note 1 This is the amount of Gross Profit calculated in the Trading Account and shown in that account as a debit entry. The credit entry in the Profit and Loss account is the double entry.

Note 2 This is the debit entry. The credit entry is in the owner or owners' Capital Account. The owner or owners of the business have invested money in the business and the net profit is the **return** on their investment in the business. The amount earned as net profit is in return for the risk they have taken investing in the business. If a business incurs a loss the **net loss** represents the amount of their Capital they have lost in the business in the financial year in which the loss was made.

Accruals and Prepayments

The figures contained in the ledger accounts are a basis from which the performance of a business is calculated at the end of a financial year. The main measure of performance is if a profit or a loss was made by a business in a financial year.

In order to calculate the profit or loss correctly for a financial year, it is necessary to **match** the **revenue earned** in the year with the **expenditure consumed**. This is known in accounting terms as the **accruals or matching** principle. Basically all this principle means is that a business may have consumed some expenses in a financial year but those expenses may not have been paid for, or expenses may have been paid for in advance and not consumed in a financial year. Two simple examples, relating to the accounts of S. Wing, will explain the concept of **accruals and prepayments**.

As we saw in the previous block, at the end of S. Wing's first year of trading which ended on 31st December 19X1, the ledger accounts were closed and the year end balances calculated. The rent payable on the shop was £400 a month, and S. Wing had only paid rent of £4,400, i.e. rent for 11 months. S. Wing's business had **consumed** 12 months worth of rent so the £400 rent owing for the month of December is treated as **rent accrued**.

In S. Wing's ledger accounts, the following entries are made to **adjust** for the £400 rent **accrued**:

Rent Account

	£		£
1st Dec 19X1 Balance c/d	4,400	31st Dec 19X1 Profit and Loss A/C (1)	4,400
31st Dec 19X1 Balance c/d	400	31st Dec 19X1 Profit and Loss A/C (2)	400
	£4,800		£4,800
		1st Jan 19X2 Balance b/d	400

Profit and Loss Account for the Year Ended 31st December, 19X1 (Extract)

	£	£
Rent (1)	4,400	
add Rent Accrued (2)	400	

As the Profit and Loss Account forms part of the double-entry system, the normal principle of **duality** applies when the Profit and Loss Account is prepared. The expense account is credited by the total expense consumed in a financial year and the Profit and Loss Account debited with that amount.

The rent accrued is **carried down (c/d)** and **brought down (b/d)** into the next financial year, i.e. 1st January 19X2 to 31st December 19X2. When the £400 owed by S. Wing is paid, the entry will be cancelled in the Rent Account. The £400 payment will be debited to the Rent Account and this will cancel out the credit balance brought forward. The credit entry will be in the Cash Account.

The rent accrued, the £400 owed by S. Wing to the owner of his shop premises, appears in the Balance Sheet under the heading of **current liabilities** as a separate item **accruals**, just below the entry for **creditors**.

A **prepayment** is dealt with in a similar way. S. Wing had paid rates to the local authority of £1,500 during the financial year ended on 31st December 19X1. The £1,500 is for rates charged for the period 1st January 19X1 to 31st March 19X1 of £300, and for the period 1st April 19X1 to 31st March 19X2 of £1,200, as the following diagram illustrates:

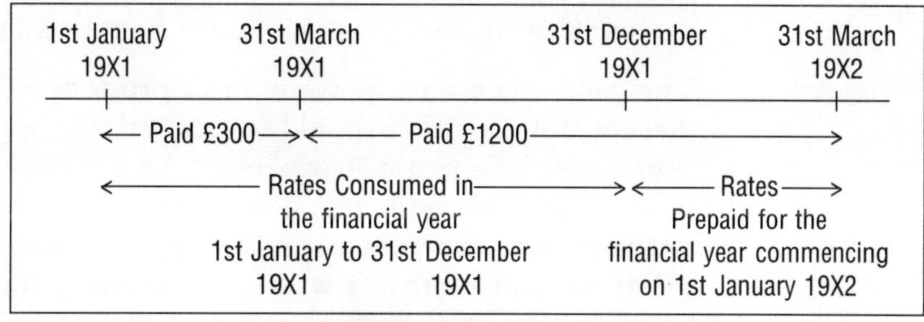

In S. Wing's ledger accounts the following entries are made to adjust for the rates prepaid:

Rates Account

	£		£
1st Dec 19X1 Balance b/d	1,500	31st Dec 19X1 Profit and Loss A/C	1,200
		31st Dec 19X1 Balance c/d	300
	£1,500		£1,500
1st Jan 19X2 Balance b/d	300		

Profit and Loss Account for the Year Ended 31st December, 19X1 (Extract)

	£		£
Rates	1,200		

The rates prepaid are **carried down (c/d)** and **brought down (b/d)** into the next financial year, i.e. 1st January 19X2 to 31st December 19X2.

The rates prepaid, the £300 **prepaid** or **paid in advance** by S. Wing to the local authority, appears in the **balance sheet** under the heading of **current assets**, as a separate item **prepayments**, just below the entry for **debtors**.

Bad Debts

During the course of trading, sooner or later goods or services will be sold on credit to a customer who may at a later date fail to pay the sum of money owed to the business. As we have already seen a **debtor** is a person or an organization who owes money to a business at a particular point in time.

If you look at the trial balance for S. Wing that was prepared in Activity 7 on page 42 you will see that there is a **debtor's account** for Vale Football Club. As you worked through Block 3 you will have seen the accounting entries made when the Treasurer of the Vale Football Club made a part payment of £500 on the £700 owing. S. Wing was told in November 19X1 that Vale Football Club has ceased to run and there was a rumour that the club had no money to pay its debts.

The basic accounting convention of **prudence** or **caution** dictates that provision should be made in the accounts in anticipation of the non-payment of the £200 owed to the business. Also the principle of **matching** revenue earned in the financial year with expenses means that the anticipated loss of £200, an expense that is written off against gross profit, must be matched with the revenue earned, the credit sale to Vale Football Club.

Bad debts are therefore amounts that are written off as an expense in the Profit and Loss Account when it is **prudent** to conclude that the money owed will not be paid. The entries in the ledger accounts to record the **write-off** of the debt of £200 owed by Vale Football Club are as follows:

Vale Football Club Account

	£		£
1st Dec 19X1 Balance b/d	200	31st Dec. 19X1 Bad Debts A/C (1)	200

Bad Debts Account

	£		£
31st Dec. 19X1 Vale Football Club A/C (1)	200	31st Dec. 19X1 Profit & Loss A/C (2)	200

Profit and Loss Account for the Year Ended 31st December 19X1 (Extract)

	£		£
Bad Debts (2)	200		

Depreciation

We have already seen that the amount of expenses consumed by a business in a financial year has to be matched with the revenue earned in that financial year. However, it is not only the expenses such as electricity and rates that are consumed by a business. The fact that trading takes place means that a proportion of the cost of fixed assets is also consumed.

S. Wing purchased a 15 year lease on his shop premises which is recorded in his ledger accounts as a **fixed asset**. At the end of 15 years the lease on the shop will have expired and will have no residual value. S. Wing will either have to negotiate with the owners of the shop premises and purchase a new lease or move to other premises.

The lease is therefore **depreciated** over a 15 year period, and following the accounting principle of **consistency** the same amount of the depreciation is charged annually to the Profit and Loss Account, as an expense, throughout the lifetime of the lease, i.e. 15 years. In this case £1,000 a year of the lease is consumed by the business, and therefore £1,000 each year is written off as an expense in the Profit and Loss Account. The following entries are made in the Ledger Accounts:

Shop Lease Account

	£		£
Cash Account	£15,000	31st Dec. 19X1 Balance c/d	£15,000
1st Jan. 19X2 Balance b/d	15,000		

Shop Lease—Provision for Depreciation Account

	£		£
31st Dec. 19X1 Balance c/d	£1,000	31st Dec. 19X1 Profit and Loss A/C	£1,000
		1st Jan. 19X2 Balance b/d	1,000

S.Wing—Profit and Loss Account for the Year Ended 31st December 19X1 (Extract)

	£		£
Depreciation—Shop lease	1,000		

In the Balance Sheet which is produced for S. Wing's business as at 31st December 19X1, the following entry will be made:

Fixed Assets	Cost	Depreciation	WDV
Shop Lease	£15,000	£1,000	£14,000

The £14,000 represents the **written down value** of the shop lease in S. Wing's ledger; this is sometimes referred to as the **book value**.

The depreciation of S. Wing's Shop Lease is an example of the **straight line** method or **fixed instalment method** of depreciation applied to a fixed asset with no **residual value**. A shop lease is a fixed asset that depreciates with the **passage of time**. Some fixed assets depreciate with use, a motor vehicle for example.

During his first year of trading S. Wing purchased a motor van from a friend for £5,000. This van is used in the business to deliver goods and collect stock from local suppliers.

Fixed assets such as motor vehicles **depreciate** with use, i.e. **wear and tear**; the more miles they cover the quicker they wear out. They therefore have to be replaced after a period of time as they may become unreliable and expensive to run as parts have to be renewed.

Fixed assets such as vehicles, fixtures, fittings, machinery, and equipment are depreciated over their **estimated useful life**. The depreciation rate on this type of asset is related to its **residual value** and **estimated useful life**.

S. Wing's vehicle has an estimated useful life of 5 years and a residual value at the end of that time of £500 — that is the estimate of the money he could sell the van for in 5 years time. You may feel that £500 is a low value and the sum of money he could get for the van should be higher. The decision to opt for a low value follows the basic accounting convention of **prudence** or **caution**. Accountants always err on the side of undervaluing such things as residual values rather than risk overvaluing. By following this convention, any subsequent rise in a residual value may be treated as a pleasant surprise for the owner of a business, in contrast to the shock which would follow the discovery of an overvaluation.

The **depreciation rate**, using the **straight line** or **fixed instalment method** of depreciation, gives the annual charge to the profit and loss account as follows:

$$\frac{\text{Cost} - \text{Residual Value}}{\text{Life in Years}} = \text{Annual Depreciation charge}$$

$$\frac{5{,}000 - 500}{5} = £900$$

Some fixed assets depreciate quicker in the early years of their estimated useful life than in the later years. Each individual fixed asset will therefore have its own **depreciation profile**.

Another method of depreciation is known as the **diminishing balance method** or **reducing balance method**, in which the written down value of the asset is reduced by a different amount each year. For example, S. Wing's motor van could be depreciated at a rate of 30% per annum as follows:

	£
Year 1 cost	5,000
Less Depreciation at 30%	1,500
Year 2 written down value	3,500
Less Depreciation at 30%	1,050
Year 3 written down value	2,450
Less Depreciation at 30%	735
	1,715
	etc

The **depreciation rate** used if this method is applied is therefore the rate which accurately reflects the Depreciation Profile of the fixed asset and its anticipated residual value. Accountants will adhere to the accounting principle of **consistency**, and once a method and rate of depreciation is adopted it will be applied over the lifetime of the asset.

You may be wondering why assets are recorded in the ledger accounts at cost. For instance, S. Wing purchased his motor van off a friend for £5,000 and could have sold it next day for £5,500. However, the motor van is recorded in the ledger account at £5,000 because the standard accounting principle known as the **cost concept** is applied. This principle states that all assets should be kept in the books at cost unless a substantial reason exists for them to be revalued. Such a **revaluation** might occur in the case of land and buildings, which in addition to being a very secure asset, tend to rise in value.

Trading and Profit and Loss Account Preparation—A Worked Example

The ledger accounts of S. Wing maintained during his first year of trading are reproduced below. For simplicity, and to stop the accounts becoming too cluttered, no entries are shown for

December 19X1, when of course in reality there would be entries to record such things as the purchase of stock and the receipt of cash for sales.

Capital Account

	£		£
31st Dec. 19X1 Drawings A/C (20)	8,800	1st Dec. 19X1 Balance b/d	25,000
31st Dec. 19X1 Balance c/d	37,505	31st Dec. 19X1 Profit & Loss A/C (19)	21,305
	£46,305		£46,305
		1st Jan. 19X2 Balance b/d	£37,505

Cash Account

	Cash £	Bank £		Cash £	Bank £
1st Dec. 19X1 Balance b/d	255	4,600	1st Dec. 19X1 Balance c/d	255	4,600
1st Jan. 19X2 Balance b/d	255	4,600			

Purchases Account

	£		£
1st Dec. Balance b/d	96,000	31st Dec. 19X1 Trading A/C (1)	96,000

Sports Equipment Supplies Account

	£		£
1st Jan. 19X1 c/d	3,200	1st Dec. 19X1 Balance b/d	3,200
		1st Jan. 19X2 Balance b/d	3,200

Shop Lease Account

	£		£
1st Dec. 19X1 Balance b/d	15,000	31st Dec. 19X1 Balance c/d	15,000
1st Jan. 19X2 Balance b/d	15,000		

Fixtures & Fittings Account

	£		£
1st Dec. 19X1 Balance b/d	2,500	31st Dec. 19X1 Balance c/d	2,500
1st Jan. 19X2 Balance b/d	2,500		

Stationery Account

	£		£
1st Dec. 19X1 Balance b/d	205	31st Dec. 19X1 Profit & Loss A/C (13)	205

Sales Account

	£		£
31st Dec. 19X1 Trading A/C (2)	114,800	1st Dec. 19X1 Balance b/d	114,800

Vale Football Club Account

	£		£
1st Dec. Balance b/d	200	31st Dec. 19X1 Bad Debts A/C (8)	200

S. Wing—Drawings Account

	£		£
1st Dec. 19X1 Balance b/d	8,800	31st Dec. Capital A/C (20)	8,800

Rates Account

	£		£
1st Dec. 19X1 Balance b/d	1,500	31st Dec. 19X1 Profit & Loss A/C (7)	1,200
		31st Dec. 19X1 Balance c/d	300
	£1,500		£1,500
1st Jan. 19X2 Balance b/d	300		

Insurance Account

	£		£
1st Dec. 19X1 Balance b/d	290	31st Dec. 19X1 Profit & Loss A/C (14)	290

Electricity Account

	£		£
1st Dec. 19X1 Balance b/d	1,200	31st Dec. 19X1 Profit & Loss A/C (15)	1,200

Telephone Account

	£		£
1st Dec. 19X1 Balance b/d	600	31st Dec. 19X1 Profit & Loss A/C (16)	600

Advertising Account

	£		£
1st Dec. 19X1 Balance b/d	1,050	31st Dec. 19X1 Profit & Loss A/C (17)	1,050

Motor Van Account

	£		£
1st Dec. 19X1 Balance b/d	5,000	1st Dec. 19X1 Balance c/d	5,000
1st Jan. 19X2 Balance b/d	5,000		

Rent Account

	£		£
1st Dec. 19X1 Balance b/d	4,400	31st Dec. 19X1 (5) Profit & Loss A/C	4,400
31st Dec. 19X1 Balance c/d	400	31st Dec. 19X1 (6) Profit & Loss A/C	400
	£4,800		£4,800
		1st Jan. 19X2 Balance b/d	400

Vehicle Running Expenses Account

	£		£
1st Dec. 19X1 Balance b/d	800	31st Dec. 19X1 Profit & Loss A/C (18)	800

Castle Golf Club Account

	£		£
1st Dec. 19X1 Balance b/d	600	31st Dec. 19X1 Balance c/d	600
1st Jan. 19X2 Balance b/d	600		

The first stage is the preparation of the Trading Account. The format was described earlier in this block, the entries are numbered for ease of identification. In practice the Folio Column in the various ledger accounts would be used to cross reference the entries that are made.

S. Wing—Trading Account for the Year Ending 31st December 19X1

	£		£
Purchases (1)	96,000	Sales (2)	114,800
Gross Profit (4)	33,800	Closing Stock (3)	15,000
	£129,800		£129,800

As already stated the closing stock is written into the books at a value of £15,000. The entries are number (3).

Stock Account

	£		
31st Dec. 19X1 Trading A/C (3)	15,000		

The trading account is balanced off and the Gross Profit of £33,800 is debited to this account and credited to the Profit and Loss Account (4).

S. Wing—Profit and Loss Account for the Year Ended 31st December 19X1 (Extract)

	£		£
		Gross Profit (4)	33,800

The next stage in the process is to make the appropriate adjustments and provisions in the ledger accounts for accruals and prepayments, bad debts, and depreciation. As discussed earlier in this block, the following adjustments and provisions have to be made to S. Wing's ledger accounts as at 31st December 19X1:

	£
a Rent accrued	400
b Rates prepaid	300
c Bad debts written off—Vale Football Club	200
d Depreciation :	
Shop lease	1,000
Motor van	900
Fixtures and fittings	250

To complete the ledger account entries for these adjustments and provisions, it is necessary to open four ledger accounts as follows:

Bad Debts Account

	£		£
31st Dec. 19X1 Vale Football A/C (8)	200	31st Dec. 19X1 Profit & Loss A/C (9)	200

Shop Lease—Provision for Depreciation Account

	£		£
31st Dec. 19X1 Balance c/d	1,000	31st Dec. 19X1 Profit & Loss A/C (10)	1,000
		1st Jan. 19X2 Balance b/d	1,000

Motor Van—Provision for Depreciation Account

	£		£
31st Dec. 19X1 Balance c/d	900	31st Dec. 19X1 Profit & Loss A/C (11)	900
		1st Jan. 19X2 Balance b/d	900

Fixtures and Fittings—Provision for Depreciation Account

	£		£
31st Dec. 19X1 Balance c/d	250	31st Dec. 19X1 Profit & Loss A/C (12)	250
		1st Jan. 19X2 Balance b/d	250

The next stage in the process of completing the Profit and Loss Account is to complete the entries for the adjustments and provisions, and then to **close off** all the **nominal** accounts and transfer the balances as at 31st December 19X1 to the Profit and Loss Account. These entries are numbered 5 to 19.

Activity 1

Follow the process of completing the Profit and Loss Account for S. Wing for the financial year ended 31st December 19X1. The numbers are there to guide you through the process.

List the accounts not included in the process and the accounts with all the **balances carried down** under the headings of **real accounts, nominal accounts**, and **personal accounts.**

S. Wing—Profit and Loss Account for the year ended 31st December 19X1

	£		£
Rent (5)	4,400	Gross Profit (4)	33,800
Rent Accrued (6)	400		
Rates (7)	1,200		
Bad Debts (9)	200		
Depreciation:			
Shop Lease (10)	1,000		
Motor Van (11)	900		
Fixtures & Fittings (12)	250		
Stationery (13)	205		
Insurance (14)	290		
Electricity (15)	1,200		
Telephone (16)	600		
Advertising (17)	1,050		
Vehicle Running Expenses (18)	800		
Net Profit (19)	21,305		
	£33,800		£33,800

The balance on the Profit and Loss Account of £21,305 is the **net profit for the year**. The credit entry is to S. Wing's Capital Account—this is the amount earned by S. Wing in his first financial year, and is the return on his investment of £25,000 and for all the work he has done throughout the year. The balance on S. Wing's Drawings Account is transferred to the Capital Account (transaction number 20). This is the amount S. Wing has drawn out of the business for his personal use during the financial year.

The list of accounts you should have drawn up in Activity 1 is:

Real Accounts	**Personal Accounts**
Cash	Sports Equipment Supplies
Shop Lease	Castle Golf Club
Fixtures and Fittings	
Motor van	
Stock	

Nominal Accounts
Capital
Rates
Rent
Provision for Depreciation:
  Shop Lease
  Motor van
  Fixtures and Fittings

The balances on these accounts are the basis for the preparation of a **Balance Sheet as at 31st December 19X1**. Balance Sheets are covered in detail in the next block.

Trading and Profit and Loss Account for Reporting and Information

We have seen the preparation of the Trading Account and Profit and Loss Account as part of a double entry book-keeping system. From the interviews in Block 2 we are aware that information which measures the performance of a business is required not only by the owner or owners of the business, but by other individuals and organizations such as banks, the Inland Revenue, creditors, and potential creditors. In order to present accounting information which is **readable** and easily **understood**, particularly by individuals who have no knowledge of accounting, the Trading and Profit and Loss Accounts are laid out in either **conventional format** or in **narrative format**. The narrative form is also referred to as the vertical format.

There are no real problems involved in the preparation of a Trading and Profit and Loss Account in either of these two formats. As an illustration, the Trading and Profit and Loss Account of S. Wing for the year ended 31st December 19X1 are presented in each format on the next 2 pages.

The Conventional Format

S. Wing—Trading and Profit and Loss Account for the year ended 31st December, 19X1

	£	£		£
Opening Stock		—	Sales	114,800
add Purchases		96,000		
		96,000		
less Closing Stock		15,000		
Cost of Goods Sold		81,000		
Gross Profit c/d		33,800		
		114,800		114,800
Rent	4,400		**Gross Profit** b/d	33,800
add Rent Accrued	400	4,800		
Rates		1,200		
Bad Debts		200		
Stationery		205		
Insurance		290		
Electricity		1,200		
Telephone		600		
Advertising		1,050		
Vehicle Running Expenses		800		
Depreciation:				
Shop Lease	1,000			
Motor Van	900			
Fixtures and Fittings	250	2,150		
Net Profit		21,305		
		£33,800		£33,800

It is one of the accounting traditions that depreciation is the last expense item listed.

As you can see the **cost of goods sold** can be ascertained using this format but the total expenses figure is not highlighted.

The Narrative or Vertical Format

S. Wing—Trading and Profit and Loss Account for the year ended 31st December, 19X1

	£	£
Sales		114,800
less **Cost of Goods Sold**		
opening stock	—	
add purchases	96,000	
	96,000	
less Closing Stock	15,000	81,000
Gross Profit		33,800
less **Expenses**		
Rent	4,800	
Rates	1,200	
Bad Debts	200	
Stationery	205	
Insurance	290	
Electricity	1,200	
Telephone	600	
Advertising	1,050	
Vehicle Running Expenses	800	
Depreciation	2,150	12,495
Net Profit		21,305

The production of the Profit and Loss Account in this format highlights sales, cost of goods sold, gross profit, total expenses, and net profit. It is important that accounting information produced is understood by the user of that information and that the main figures are highlighted, as they are in this narrative or vertical format.

Dealing with a Loss in a Financial Year

S. Wing earned a profit of £21,305 in his first year of trading but he could have had a bad year and **incurred** a loss. Some businesses will make a loss in a bad year, but in general this is uncommon. Normally if a business is running at a loss the owner or owners will soon become aware of it as they will experience a fall in sales and cash shortages, and very often cease to trade after a period if the trading position does not look like improving.

Activity 2

Assume that during S. Wing's first year of trading his sales are only £90,000 and all other items—purchases, stock, and expenses—are the same as in the examples above.

a Draw up a Trading and Profit and Loss Account for the year ended 31st March, 19X2 in narrative format.

b List the various reasons why a business may incur a loss.

S. Wing made a loss of £3,495. In S. Wing's ledger accounts the loss is recorded as follows:

S. Wing—Profit and Loss Account for year ended 31st December 19X1 (Extract)

	£		£
		Net Loss	3,495

S. Wing—Capital Account

	£		£
31st Dec. 19X1 profit and loss A/C	3,495	1st Dec. 19X1 Balance b/d	25,000

The amount of capital S. Wing has invested in the business is therefore reduced by the loss of £3,495 incurred.

Preparation of a Trading and Profit and Loss Account from a Trial Balance

We saw in the previous block how a Trial Balance is prepared at the end of a financial year. As the Trial Balance is a list of all the balances in the ledger accounts, it is a basis for the preparation of the Trading and Profit and Loss Account. In practice, a Trading and Profit and Loss Account is prepared from the Trial Balance, and the appropriate double-entries are made in the ledger accounts when the Trial Balance is prepared. The Trial Balance also forms the basis for the preparation of the **Balance Sheet** as we shall see in the next block.

The Production of a Trial Balance and Profit and Loss Account using an Accounting Package

As discussed in Block 3, accounting packages are able to produce detailed accounting information for each month and at the end of a financial year.

When using a typical package, you select the Management Reports Option from the main menu and, by inserting the appropriate commands, a Trial Balance and Profit and Loss Account can be produced.

The following is a print-out of the Trial Balance and Profit and Loss Account for S. Wing as at 31st December 19X1 as it would look when produced using an accounting package.

Please note that the 31st December 19X1 is shown as 311291. Figures for the month of December have been omitted. In practice a Trial Balance and a Profit and Loss Account would be produced at the end of each month.

Ref	Account Name	Debit	Credit
0001	Shop Lease	15000.00	
0002	Acc.Deprec'n - Shop Lease		1000.00
0003	Motor Van	5000.00	
0004	Acc.Deprec'n - Motor Van		900.00
0005	Fixtures & Fittings	2500.00	
0006	Acc.Deprec'n - Fix's & Fitt's		250.00
0037	Stock on Hand	15000.00	
0038	Debtor's Control	600.00	
0039	Prepayments	300.00	
0065	Creditor's Control		3200.00
0066	Accruals		400.00
0088	Cash	255.00	
0089	Bank	4600.00	
0090	Capital Invested - S. Wing		25000.00
0091	Drawings - S. Wing	8800.00	
1001	Sales		114800.00
2001	Purchases	96000.00	
2003	Closing Stock		15000.00
3001	Rent	4800.00	
3002	Rates	1200.00	
3003	Bad Debts	200.00	
3004	Stationery	205.00	
3005	Insurance	290.00	
3006	Electricity	1200.00	
3007	Telephone	600.00	
3008	Advertising	1050.00	
3009	Vehicle Running Expenses	800.00	
3101	Deprec'n - Shop Lease	1000.00	

3102	Deprec'n - Motor Van	900.00	
3103	Deprec'n - Fix's & Fitt's	250.00	
		160550.00	160550.00

S. WING Management Reports - Profit & Loss Account Date: 311291
Page: 1

	This Month		Year to Date	
Sales				
Sports Equipment	114800.00		114800.00	
		114800.00		114800.00
Purchases				
Sports Equipment	96000.00		96000.00	
Less Closing Stock	(15000.00)		(15000.00)	
		81000.00		81000.00
	Gross Profit	33800.00	Gross Profit	33800.00
Overheads				
Rent	4800.00		4800.00	
Rates	1200.00		1200.00	
Bad Debts	200.00		200.00	
Stationery	205.00		205.00	
Insurance	290.00		290.00	
Electricity	1200.00		1200.00	
Telephone	600.00		600.00	
Advertising	1050.00		1050.00	
Vehicle Running Expenses	800.00		800.00	
Deprec'n - Shop Lease	1000.00		1000.00	
Deprec'n - Motor Van	900.00		900.00	
Deprec'n - Fix's & Fitt's	250.00		250 00	
		12495.00		12495.00
	Net Profit	21305.00	Net Profit	21305.00

Activity 3

The following Trial Balance relates to the business activities of S. Wing during the financial year ending 31st December 19X2. Using the information it contains and making the appropriate provisions and adjustments required, prepare a Trading and Profit and Loss Account for the year ended 31st December 19X2 in a format you think suitable for presentation to a Bank Manager.

S. Wing—Trial Balance as at 31st December 19X2

Account	Debit	Credit
	£	£
Capital		37,505
Cash at Bank	14,000	
Cash in Hand	535	
Purchases	102,000	
Stock in Hand on 1st January, 19X2	15,000	
Sports Equipment Supplies Ltd.		7,450
Shop lease	15,000	
Shop lease—Provision for Depreciation		1,000
Fixtures and Fittings	7,500	
Fixtures and Fittings—Provision for Depreciation		250
Stationery	450	
Sales		134,700
Drawings	9,800	
Rates	1,550	
Insurance	340	
Electricity	1,700	
Telephone	700	
Advertising	1,510	
Motor Van	5,000	
Motor Van—Provision for Depreciation		900
Rent	4,400	
Motor Van Running Expenses	700	
Castle Golf Club	900	
Red Lion Football Club	300	
Repairs and Maintenance	420	
	£181,805	£181,805

Notes

1 Stock in hand on 31st December 19X2 was £22,000.

2 Rates prepaid on 31st December 19X2 were £350.

3 Rent accrued on 31st December 19X2 was £400.

4 Depreciation is to be provided for the year ended 31st December 19X2 as follows:

Shop lease	£1,000
Motor Van	£900
Fixtures and fittings	£700

Summary

This block has discussed the processes involved in the preparation of a Trading and Profit and Loss Account for a business. It must be emphasized that the basic information for completing this process is the various ledger accounts. It is of fundamental importance therefore for these accounts to be maintained as accurately as possible.

The format of the Trading and Profit and Loss Account needs careful consideration, and the choice must be related to the needs of the user or users and their level of knowledge of accounting.

The way in which accounting information is produced and presented is therefore very important, and we shall continue this theme in the next block on Balance Sheets.

Block 5
The Balance Sheet

Introduction

The last two blocks described the maintenance of ledger accounts to record the financial transactions of a business. They also detailed how the balances on these accounts are used as the basis for the production of accounting information to measure the performance of a business in terms of the **profit earned** or **loss incurred** in a financial year.

As we have seen in the previous block, not all the ledger accounts are used as a basis for the preparation of the Profit and Loss Account; we identified accounts, such as the Motor Van Account and the Fixtures and Fitting Account, which are used to maintain a record of the **cost** or **worth** of an asset used in a business.

The Balance Sheet is a document which is produced to show the **worth** of a business at a particular point in time. It can be produced at any time but normally a Balance Sheet is produced at the end of a trading period, a financial year, and shows its **financial position as at** that point in time.

A Balance Sheet is therefore a **snapshot** of the financial position or **worth** of a business at a particular point in time, **as at** midnight on a particular date.

The Balance Sheet Equation

The Balance Sheet shows what a business owns in the form of **assets** and what it **owes** in the form of **liabilities**.

The **assets** which a business owns will of course depend on the nature of the business.

Activity 1

List the assets that will be owned by the following business organizations:

a A sole trader who owns and runs a garage which sells petrol and diesel and which has a workshop for the repair and servicing of vehicles, located in a small village.

b A partnership of three people who run and own a garden centre on the outskirts of a large town.

c A private limited company which manufactures a range of sports bags which it sells and delivers direct to sports shops.

d A public limited company which manufactures high class motor vehicles and jet engines.

Similarly, the liabilities of a business organization will depend on the structure of that business, how it is financed, and the nature of the business carried out.

Activity 2

List the liabilities for each of the business organizations referred to in Activity 1. To complete this activity you may have to refer to Block 1 which described the sources of capital for each type of business organization.

A business organization may have financed its operations from a variety of sources, such as from the use of a sole trader's own capital, the raising of loans, or the issue of shares. The money raised is used to finance the purchase of assets which are **employed** in the business.

If an owner of a business uses his own money to start a business then this is **capital**. Even if the ownership of a business is shared between a group of people, such as in a partnership, if each partner **injects** some of his own money to set up a business or to expand it then the concept is the same.

The injecting of capital or the raising of loans to finance business operations is termed **long-term financing**. A business can also finance its operations in the **short term** by paying for goods on credit, and by bank overdrafts.

The basic Balance Sheet Equation is:

assets = liabilities

As we saw in the previous block, assets are classified either as **fixed assets** or **current assets**.

Fixed assets are items owned by the business which will be consumed by the business over a period of more than one financial year. They include land, buildings, and motor vehicles.

Current assets are items owned by the business which will be consumed by the business over a period of less than one financial year. They include stock, debtors, and cash.

The Balance Sheet equation can therefore be expressed as:

fixed assets + current assets = liabilities

Similarly liabilities can be classified either as **capital** or **current liabilities.**

Capital is the amount of money used to finance the business and is owed to the owners of the business.

Current liabilities are items owed by the business which will be repaid by the business over a period of less than one financial year; they include creditors and bank overdrafts.

The Balance Sheet equation can therefore be expressed as:

fixed assets + current assets = capital + current liabilities

A business may have financed its operations by raising long-term loans—loans repayable by the business over a period of more than one financial year—from a bank or other financial institution. If a business has financed the purchase of assets in this way the Balance Sheet Equation is expressed as:

fixed assets + current assets = capital + long term liabilities + current liabilities

This simple equation or relationship is the basis of financial reporting. A simple illustration will show how this equation operates.

In Block 3 we discussed the various financial transactions that were involved in the setting up of S. Wing's business. As already described, a Balance Sheet is a **snapshot** of the financial worth or the financial position of a business at a particular point in time. Therefore a Balance Sheet could be produced after each financial transaction.

a S. Wing commenced trading on 1st January 19X1. He transferred £25,000 from his private bank account to a business bank account he had opened at a local bank.

If a Balance Sheet was produced after this transaction it would show:

Assets	£	**Liabilities**	£
Cash at Bank	£25,000	Capital	£25,000

b On the same day, he took delivery of stock of golfing equipment and sports goods from Sports Equipment Supplies Ltd. The cost of this stock was £10,000 and S. Wing agreed to pay the invoice for these goods at the end of the following month.

If a Balance Sheet was produced after this transaction it would show:

Assets	£	**Liabilities**	£
Stock	10,000	Capital	25,000
Cash at Bank	25,000	Creditor	10,000
	£35,000		£35,000

Notice how the assets of the business have increased by £10,000 but this is offset by the increase of £10,000 in liabilities.

c Also on the same day he wrote a cheque for £15,000 and paid the owner of the shop premises for a 15 year lease.

Assets	£	**Liabilities**	£
Shop Lease	15,000	Capital	25,000
Stock	10,000	Creditor	10,000
Cash at Bank	10,000		
	£35,000		£35,000

As the volume of transactions increases, and S. Wing expands his business by buying more stock and equipment, there will be an increase in assets and liabilities and the Balance Sheet or business situation will become more complicated. The important point however is that the basic concept of the Balance Sheet equation remains the same:

assets = liabilities

The assets and liabilities produced in the Balance Sheet above are presented under the different classifications as follows:

S. Wing—Balance Sheet as at 1st January 19X1

	£	£		£
Fixed Assets			**Capital**	25,000
Shop lease		15,000		
Current Assets			**Current Liabilities**	
Stock	10,000		Creditors	10,000
Cash at bank	10,000	20,000		
		£35,000		£35,000

This is S. Wing's Balance Sheet as at midnight on 1st January 19X1. It shows his financial position at that point in time and details his assets and liabilities.

The following shows S. Wing's Balance Sheet as at 31st January 19X1 as it would look if it had been produced using a typical accounting package. Please note that the 31st January 19X1 is shown as 310191.

A Balance Sheet can be produced at any time. The facilities provided in a typical accounting package allow the user to produce a Balance Sheet at the end of each month. Page 78 shows S. Wing's Balance Sheet as at 31st December 19X1. Please note that the 31st December 19X1 is shown as 311291.

S. WING A:\MENU Management Reports - Balance Sheet Date: 310191
Page: 1

	This Month		Year to Date	
Fixed Assets				
Shop Lease		15000.00		15000.00
Fixtures & Fittings		500.00		500.00
		15500.00		15500.00
Current Assets				
Debtors	900.00		900.00	
Bank	13750.00		13750.00	
Cash	200.00		200.00	
	14850.00		14850.00	
Current Liabilities				
Creditors	10000.00		10000.00	
	10000.00		10000.00	
Net Current Assets		4850.00		4850.00
Total Assets less Current Liabilities		20350.00		20350.00

Financed by				
Capital Invested - S. Wing	25000.00		25000.00	
Drawings - S. Wing	(500.00)		(500.00)	
Profit/Loss Account	(4150.00)		(4150.00)	
		20350.00		20350.00
		========		========

S. WING A:\MENU Management Reports - Balance Sheet Date: 311291
Page: 1

	This Month		Year to Date	
Fixed Assets				
Shop Lease		14000.00		14000.00
Motor Van		4100.00		4100.00
Fixtures & Fittings		2250.00		2250.00
		20350.00		20350.00
Current Assets				
Stock	15000.00		15000.00	
Debtors	600.00		600.00	
Prepayments	300.00		300.00	
Bank	4600.00		4600.00	
Cash	255.00		255.00	
	20755.00		20755.00	
Current Liabilities				
Creditors	3200.00		3200.00	
Accruals	400.00		400.00	
	3600.00		3600.00	
Net Current Assets		17155.00		17155.00
Total Assets less Current Liabilities		37505.00		37505.00
		========		========

```
Financed by

Capital Invested - S. Wing 25000.00          25000.00
Drawings - S. Wing        (8800.00)          (8800.00)
Profit/Loss Account        21305.00)          21305.00)
                                     ________            ________
                                     37505.00            37505.00
                                     ========            ========
```

The Balance Sheet: a Worked Example

The trial balance of S. Wing as at 31st December 19X2 was as follows:

Account	*Debit*	*Credit*
	£	£
Capital		37,505
Cash at Bank	14,000	
Cash in hand	535	
Purchases	102,000	
Stock in hand 1st January 19X2	15,000	
Sports Equipment Supplies Ltd		7,450
Shop lease	15,000	
Shop lease—Provision for Depreciation		1,000
Fixtures and Fittings	7,500	
Fixtures and Fittings—Provision for depreciation		250
Stationery	450	
Sales		134,700
Drawings	9,800	
Rates	1,550	
Insurance	340	
Electricity	1,700	
Telephone	700	
Advertising	1,510	
Motor Van	5,000	
Motor Van—Provision for Depreciation		900
Rent	4,400	
Motor Van Running Expenses	700	
Castle Golf Club	900	
Red Lion Football Club	300	
Repairs and maintenance	420	
	£181,805	£181,805

On page 71 you prepared the Trading and Profit and Loss Account for the year ended 31st December 19X2 as follows:

S. Wing—Trading and Profit and Loss Account for the Year Ended 31st December 19X2

	£	£
Sales		134,700
less **Cost of goods sold**		
Opening stock	15,000	
add Purchases	102,000	
	117,000	
less Closing stock	22,000	95,000
Gross Profit		39,700
less **Expenses**		
Stationery	450	
Rates	1,200	
Insurance	340	
Electricity	1,700	
Telephone	700	
Advertising	1,510	
Rent	4,800	
Motor Van Running Expenses	700	
Repairs and Maintenance	420	
Depreciation : Shop Lease	1,000	
Motor Van	900	
Fixtures and Fittings	700	14,420
Net Profit for the year		25,280

If you look at the Trial Balance as at 31st December 19X2 again you will see that the majority of the balances listed were used in the production of the Trading and Profit and Loss Account. The balances not used in this process were:

Account	*Debit* £	*Credit* £
Capital		37,505
Cash at bank	14,000	
Cash in Hand	535	
Sports Equipment Supplies Ltd.		7,450
Shop Lease	15,000	
Provision for Depreciation—Shop Lease		1,000
Fixtures and Fittings	7,500	
Provision for Depreciation—Fixtures & Fittings		250
Drawings	9,800	
Motor Van	5,000	
Provision for Depreciation—Motor Van		900
Castle Golf Club	900	
Red Lion Football Club	300	
	£53,035	£47,105

This of course does not balance because we have not taken account of stock, accruals and prepayments, or depreciation.

The ledger accounts of S. Wing will contain the following details in relation to the adjustments and provisions that took place on 31st December 19X2.

Stock Account

	£		£
31st Dec. 19X1 Trading A/C	15,000	31st Dec. 19X2 Trading A/C	15,000
31st Dec. 19X2 Trading A/C	22,000	31st Dec. 19X2 Balance c/d	22,000
1st Jan. 19X3 Balance b/d	22,000		

Rates Account

	£		£
31st Dec. 19X2 Balance b/d	1,550	31st Dec. 19X2 Profit & Loss A/C	1,200
		31st Dec. 19X2 Balance c/d	350
	£1,550		£1,550
1st Jan. 19X3 Balance b/d	350		

Rent Account

	£		£
31st Dec. 19X2 Balance b/d	4,400	31st Dec. 19X2 Profit & Loss A/C	4,400
31st Dec. 19X2 Balance c/d	400	31st Dec. 19X2 Profit & Loss A/C	400
	£4,800		£4,800
		1st Jan. 19X3 Balance b/d	400

Shop Lease—Provision for Depreciation Account

	£		£
31st Dec. 19X2 Balance c/d	2,000	1st Jan. 19X2 Balance b/d	1,000
		31st Dec. 19X2 Profit & Loss A/C	1,000
	£2,000		£2,000
		1st Jan. 19X3 Balance b/d	2,000

Motor Van—Provision for Depreciation Account

	£		£
		1st Jan. 19X2 Balance b/d	900
31st Dec. 19X2 Balance c/d	1,800	31st Dec. 19X2 Profit & Loss A/C	900
	£1,800		£1,800
		1st Jan. 19X3 Balance b/d	1,800

Fixtures and Fittings—Provision for Depreciation Account

	£		£
		1st Jan. 19X2 Balance b/d	250
31st Dec. 19X2 Balance c/d	950	31st Dec. 19X2 Profit & Loss A/C	700
	£950		£950
		1st Jan. 19X3 Balance b/d	950

We have also calculated the balance on the Profit and Loss Account which we have seen in Block 4 is maintained in the ledger.

Profit and Loss Account

	£		£
		31st Dec. 19X2 Balance b/d	25,280

The list of balances can now be rewritten incorporating the balances detailed above:

Account	*Debit* £	*Credit* £
Capital		37,505
Cash at Bank	14,000	
Cash in Hand	535	
Stock in Hand 31st December 19X2	22,000	
Sports Equipment Supplies Ltd.		7,450
Shop Lease	15,000	
Shop Lease—Provision for Depreciation		2,000
Fixtures and Fittings	7,500	
Fixtures & Fittings—Provision for Depreciation		950
Drawings	9,800	
Rates Prepaid	350	
Motor Van	5,000	
Motor Van—Provision for Depreciation		1,800
Rent Accrued		400
Castle Golf Club	900	
Red Lion Football Club	300	
Profit and Loss		25,280
	£75,385	£75,385

The list of balances above can be considered as a **position statement** of S. Wing's business as at 31st December 19X2. It is a list of assets and liabilities.

As we have seen, the fundamental objective of producing financial information is its presentation in a form that is both **readable** and **understandable** by the **users** of such information. Obviously the list of balances above does not fit that criteria.

Activity 3

List the people who will be interested in the financial position of the following business organizations at the end of a financial year:

a A Sole Trader who owns and runs a garage in a small village.
b A Partnership of three people who own and run a garden centre on the outskirts of a large town.
c A Private Limited Company which manufactures a range of sports bags which it sells and delivers direct to sports shops.
d A Public Limited Company which manufactures high class motor vehicles and jet engines.

As we saw in Block 4, the capital that has been **injected** into the business is used to finance the purchase of assets that are **employed** by the business. If the employment of these assets is managed efficiently then a profit will be earned.

The profit that is not consumed by the payment of expenses or taken out of the business for personal use, as **drawings**, by the owner or owners is retained in the business and thus increases the amount of capital.

In order to compile the Balance Sheet for S. Wing as at 31st December 19X2 we must transfer the profit for the year to S. Wing's Capital Account and close his Drawings Account as follows:

Capital Account

	£		£
31st Dec. 19X2 Drawings A/C	9,800	31st Jan. 19X2 Balance b/d	37,505
31st Dec. 19X2 Balance c/d	52,985	31st Dec. 19X2 Profit & Loss A/C	25,280
	£62,785		£62,785
		1st Jan. 19X3 Balance b/d	52,985

Profit and Loss Account

	£		£
31st Dec. 19X2 Capital A/C	25,280	31st Dec. 19X2 Balance b/d	25,280

S. Wing—Drawings Account

	£		£
31st Dec. 19X2 Balance b/d	9,800	31st Dec. 19X2 Capital A/C	9,800

The list of balances in the ledger accounts of S. Wing as at 31st Dec. 19X2 after all adjustments is as follows:

Account	*Debit*	*Credit*
	£	£
Capital		52,985
Cash at Bank	14,000	
Cash in Hand	535	
Stock in Hand 31st December 19X2	22,000	
Sports Equipment Supplies Ltd.		7,450
Shop Lease	15,000	
Shop Lease—Provision for Depreciation		2,000
Fixtures and Fittings	7,500	
Fixtures & Fittings—Provision for Depreciation		950
Rates Prepaid	350	
Motor Van	5,000	
Motor Van—Provision for Depreciation		1,800
Rent Accrued		400
Castle Golf Club	900	
Red Lion Football Club	300	
	£65,585	£65,585

A Balance Sheet can now be produced in a format suitable for use by the various people who are interested in the financial position of S. Wing's business. But before this can be done, the various **assets and liabilities** have to be classified under the various headings described earlier in this block.

Activity 4

Classify S. Wing's assets and liabilities listed above under the following headings:

fixed assets, current assets, capital, current liabilities

Using the Balance Sheet Equation a Balance Sheet can be produced as follows:

Assets	£	£	**Liabilities**	£	£
Fixed Assets (note 1)			**Capital**		52,985
Shop lease	13,000				
Motor van	3,200				
Fixtures & Fittings	6,550	22,750			
Current Assets			**Current Liabilities**		
Stock	22,000		Creditors (note 3)	7,450	
Debtors (note 2)	1,200		Accruals	400	7,850
Prepayments	350				
Cash in bank	14,000				
Cash in hand	535	38,085			
		£60,835			£60,835

Notes for Balance Sheet on page 84:

1 Fixed Assets figures are calculated as follows:
Cost – provision for depreciation = written down value (WDV)

2 Debtors:

	£
Castle Golf Club	900
Red Lion Football Club	300
	£1,200

3 Creditors

Sports Equipment Suppliers Ltd.	£7,450

A Balance Sheet to provide information and reports on the **financial position or worth** of a business as at the end of a **financial year** is produced in the following format:

Balance Sheet as at 31st December 19X2

	£	£	£
Fixed Assets	**Cost**	**Depreciation**	**WDV**
Detail	X	X	X
			XX
Current Assets			
Stock	X		
Debtors	X		
Prepayments	X		
Cash at Bank	X		
Cash in Hand	X	XX	
less Current Liabilities			
Creditors	X		
Accruals	X	XX	
Working Capital			XX
Capital Employed			£
Financed by:			
Capital			X
Long Term Liabilities			X
			£

Capital employed is the amount of funds circulated in the business and this concept is illustrated and discussed in the following block.

Activity 5

Produce the Balance Sheet for S. Wing's business as at 31st December 19X2 in the format shown above.

The Trading and Profit and Loss Account and Balance Sheets are used to measure the **performance and worth** of a business during a financial year and to report on the position of the business at the end of the same financial year. Performance measurement is dealt with in Block 8. In order for the accounting statements to provide information for comparison it is necessary to provide the previous financial year's figures. The accepted practice is to produce these figures in the left hand column of the statement, in the case of the Balance Sheet as follows:

S. Wing—Balance Sheet as at 31st December 19X2

As at 31st Dec. 19X1		As at 31st Dec. 19X2		
£		£	£	£
	Fixed Assets	**Cost**	**Depreciation**	**WDV**
12,000	Shop Lease	15,000	2,000	13,000
4,100	Motor Van	5,000	1,800	3,200
2,250	Fixtures and Fittings	7,500	950	6,550
18,350				22,750
	Current Assets			
15,000	Stock	22,000		
	etc.			
	etc.			

Activity 6

Using the information contained in this block on S. Wing's Trading and Profit and Loss Account and Balance Sheet as at 31st December 19X2, and the Trial Balance as at 31st December 19X3, detailed below, prepare a Trading and Profit and Loss Account for the year ended 31st March 19X3 and a Balance Sheet as at that date using comparative figures in the way previously illustrated.

S. Wing—Trial Balance as at 31st December 19X3

Account	*Debit*	*Credit*
	£	£
Capital		52,985
Cash at Bank		2,300
Cash in Hand	220	
Purchases	113,535	
Stock in Hand as at 1st Jan. 19X3	22,000	
Sports Equipment & Supplies Ltd.		9,760
Shop Lease	15,000	
Shop Lease—Provision for Depreciation		2,000
Fixtures and Fittings	7,500	
Fixtures and Fittings—Provision for Depreciation		950
Motor Van	5,000	
Motor Van—Provision for Depreciation		1,800
Wages of Shop Assistant	6,500	
Stationery	570	
Sales		118,200

Drawings	10,900	
Rates	1,200	
Insurance	360	
Electricity	1,900	
Long-term Loan		5,000
Telephone	800	
Advertising	1,920	
Rent	4,000	
Motor Van Running Expenses	800	
Red Lion Football Club	120	
Repairs and Maintenance	290	
Valley Golf Club	380	
	£192,995	£192,995

Notes

1 Stock in hand at 31st December 19X3 was £26,000.

2 Rates accrued on 31st December 19X3 was £430.

3 Rent accrued on 31st December 19X3 was £800.

4 Depreciation is to be provided for the year ended 31st December 19X3 as follows:

Shop lease	£1,000
Motor van	£900
Fixtures & Fittings	£700

Summary

In this block we have seen how a balance sheet can be presented in a format that is suitable for the purposes of **reporting** the financial position of a business as at the end of a financial year. The next block will look at the requirements for producing financial statements like these in a format that is suitable for them to be termed **published accounts**. These accounts, and the information given in them or as notes to the accounts, have to comply with various statutory guidelines such as those given in the Companies Acts, which prescribe certain formats. Essentially there is no conceptual difference between the accounts of businesses like S. Wing and the accounts produced by large public limited companies. It is only the detail that is somewhat different.

Block 6
The Accounts of Limited Companies

Introduction

In Blocks 4 and 5 we looked at the processes involved in the production of a Trading and Profit and Loss Account as a means of reporting the financial performance of a business during an accounting period. We also looked at the Balance Sheet which shows the financial position as at the final date of the accounting period.

The financial accounts that are produced for sole traders and partnerships are confidential documents to which the owners only allow access when it is required by law, for example, when the Inland Revenue requires them as a basis for assessing the tax due by the owners. In addition, individuals or institutions may require to see past accounts before they will provide the business with some service or facility; this would include a bank manager who has been asked to provide overdraft facilities.

This block looks at the accounts of limited liability companies who are required by law to produce Annual Accounts in a specified format and to deposit a copy of the accounts with the Registrar of Companies in Cardiff. The Registrar maintains a file on every company, which includes copies of Annual Accounts which are available for inspection by members of the public.

Unlike those of sole traders and partnerships, the accounts of limited liability companies are not confidential. Public limited companies (PLCs) publish an Annual Report and Financial Statements that are available to everyone; in fact PLCs use their annual report in part as a promotional aid for their business.

This block looks at the 1987 Annual Report and Financial Statements of Marks and Spencer PLC to illustrate the general principles and practices involved in the production of the Annual Accounts of a Limited Company.

The Limited Company

Block 1 described the process involved in the formation of a limited company. This type of company is the largest type of business organization in the United Kingdom. Normally the company will have a Head Office and branches that are spread throughout a region, or the country as a whole.

The Companies Act, 1985, governs the activities of limited companies by regulating both the formation and conduct of the companies with a view to protecting investors and creditors.

A company's Memorandum of Association will contain details of the **share capital** and the amount of this that the company is authorized to issue. The shares of a **private limited company** are not available for sale to the general public whereas the shares of a **public limited company (PLC)** can be purchased by anyone. Trading in the shares of a PLC is carried out on the **Stock Exchange** and the price of the shares is published daily in the Financial Times and other newspapers.

The Memorandum of Association of a PLC contains a statement that it is in fact a PLC and that it has a minimum **share capital** of £50,000.

The owners of a company are known as **members** or **shareholders**. The capital of a company is usually divided into **ordinary** and **preference shares** and each member of a company will own a number of shares depending upon how much they wish to invest in the company.

The Companies Act, 1985, requires a company to hold an **annual general meeting** where the members elect the **directors** who will run the business on their behalf. This gives us the concept of **stewardship**. The Directors of a company prepare an **Annual Report** on their stewardship to the members, and they are also charged with the responsibility of reporting on the financial affairs of the company. Therefore, in addition to the Annual Report on their **management stewardship** they also present to the members **annual financial statements**—this is the concept of **financial stewardship**. A copy of the report of the Directors of Marks and Spencer PLC is reproduced overleaf:

MARKS AND SPENCER p.l.c.

Report of the Directors

The directors have pleasure in submitting their report and the financial statements of the Company and its subsidiaries for the year ended 31 March 1987.

Principal activities

Retailing

The Group sells clothing, household goods and foods under the St Michael trade mark in its chain of stores in the United Kingdom, France, Belgium and Ireland. It also sells a range of St Michael merchandise and other consumer goods through a chain of stores in Canada and has opened its first store under the D'Allaird's name, in the United States of America. St Michael merchandise is also sold for export.

Financial activities

These comprise the operation of the Marks and Spencer Chargecard together with leasing and insurance activities.

Review of activities

The year ended 31 March 1987.

The Group continued to expand its activities during the year.

In the United Kingdom the Company opened its first edge-of-town store at the Metro Centre in Gateshead and a further seven satellite stores, and now has a total of 274 outlets. Together with extensions at existing stores, sales area has now increased from 7,486,000 square feet to 7,942,000 square feet.

In Europe a new store was opened in the Paris region bringing the total number of European stores to 10.

The minority interest in the Canadian subsidiary was acquired in June 1986.

The Canadian subsidiary now has 262 stores compared with 243 last year and total sales floor footage has increased from 2,394,000 square feet to 2,541,000 square feet.

In March 1987 the Group opened its first American store, under the D'Allaird's name, at Watertown, New York State. The second store opened in April in Albany, New York State.

The Marks and Spencer Chargecard is operating successfully. There are now some 1·5 million cards in circulation and sales through the card continue to increase.

St Michael Financial Services has obtained a licence from the Bank of England enabling it to operate as a licensed deposit taker.

Future developments

The Group will continue to expand into new areas of merchandise where these are considered appropriate and plans to continue its physical expansion. In the United Kingdom, our capital expenditure for the year to 31 March 1988, mainly relating to new stores and extensions, is expected to be in the region of £350 million. In June 1987 St Michael Financial Services will be acquiring the Marks and Spencer Budget Account which is presently owned and administered by Citibank Savings.

A small group of senior people now resident in New York is investigating future development opportunities in the USA.

Profit and dividends

The profit for the financial year as shown in the financial statements amounted to £276·0 million. The directors recommend that this be dealt with as follows:

Dividends	£m
Preference shares	0·1
Ordinary shares: Interim dividend paid, 1·4p per share (last year 1·25p)	37·1
Final dividend proposed, 3·1p per share (last year 2·65p)	82·3
Total ordinary dividends, 4·5p per share (last year 3·9p)	119·4
Undistributed surplus	156·5
	276·0

The proposed final dividend will be paid on 17 July 1987 to shareholders whose names are on the Register of Members at the close of business on 22 May 1987.

Directors

The present directors of the Company are shown on pages 2 and 3.

In accordance with Article 85 of the Company's Articles of Association, Mr J A Lusher, Mr J K Oates, Mr S J Sacher and Mr D G Trangmar retire by rotation and, being eligible, offer themselves for re-election.

Dr D V Atterton was appointed as a non-executive director on 1 January 1987 and Mr D G Lanigan was appointed as a non-executive director on 6 April 1987. They retire in accordance with Article 91 of the Company's Articles of Association and, being eligible, offer themselves for re-election.

Mr W B Howard retired on 31 March 1987.

Directors' interests in shares and debentures

The beneficial interests of the directors and their families in the shares of the Company and its subsidiaries, together with their interests as trustees of both charitable and other trusts, are shown in note 21 on page 46. Further information regarding share options is given in note 8 on page 36.

Transactions with directors

Directors' interests in contracts or arrangements with the Company during the year are shown in note 20 on page 45.

Ordinary share capital

During the year ended 31 March 1987, 8,141,768 ordinary shares in the Company were issued as follows:

a 3,310,496 to the Trustees of the United Kingdom Employees' Profit Sharing Schemes at 210p each, in respect of the allocation from the profits of the year ended 31 March 1986.
b 1,232,720 under the terms of the 1977 United Kingdom Senior Staff Share Option Scheme (as adjusted for scrip issue in July 1984) at prices between 61·175p and 107·475p each.
c 3,598,552 under the terms of the United Kingdom Employees' Savings-Related Share Option Scheme.

At 6 May 1987, Prudential Corporation p.l.c. and its subsidiaries held 169,005,723 ordinary shares which represented 6·4% of the issued ordinary share capital of the Company. The Company has not received notification that any other person held more than 5·0% of the issued ordinary share capital.

United Kingdom employees' profit sharing schemes

The amount of profit which will be allocated this year in the form of ordinary shares in the Company has been fixed at £9·0 million, representing 4·75% of the earnings of 27,039 eligible employees.

Employee involvement

We have maintained our commitment to employee involvement.

Staff are kept well informed of the performance and objectives of the Company through established methods of personal briefings and regular meetings. These are supplemented by our staff newspaper, *St Michael News* and video presentations.

Communication Groups in stores and warehouses are meetings of management with elected representatives of the staff. They are chaired by a member of staff. These Groups provide an opportunity for staff to contribute to the everyday running of their workplace. They also ensure an additional channel for comments on Company-wide issues as minutes of meetings are circulated to Divisional management and Head Office.

Directors and executives regularly visit stores and discuss with members of the staff matters of current interest and concern to the business. Staff representatives attend the annual general meetings and all members of the staff have the Group results explained in *St Michael News*.

We have long-established Employees' Profit Sharing and Savings-Related Option Schemes, memberships of which are service related. All the Company's share schemes are offered for renewal during 1987/88.

Disabled employees

We have continued our policy of giving disabled people full and fair consideration for all job vacancies for which they offer themselves as suitable applicants, having regard to their particular aptitudes and abilities. Training and career development opportunities are available to all employees and if necessary we endeavour to re-train any member of staff who develops a disability during employment with us.

Charitable and political contributions

Direct donations to charitable organisations amounted to £1,218,000. A political contribution was made to British United Industrialists of £50,000.

Exports

The value of goods exported directly from the United Kingdom, including shipments to overseas subsidiaries, amounted to £115·1 million (last year £106·3 million).

Resolution Number 10 — an explanation

The Companies Act 1985 prevents the directors of a company from allotting unissued shares without the authority of the shareholders in general meeting. In certain circumstances, this could unduly restrict the directors from carrying on the Company's business to best advantage.

Authority is therefore sought for your directors to be able to allot unissued shares if it became beneficial to the Company to do so, subject to the limitations set out in the Resolution.

The Stock Exchange no longer requires shareholder consent to each allotment of shares for cash made otherwise than to existing shareholders in proportion to their existing shareholdings, subject to shareholders approving this Resolution.

Income and Corporation Taxes Act 1970

The close company provisions of this Act do not apply to the Company.

Auditors

A resolution proposing the reappointment of Deloitte Haskins & Sells as auditors to the Company will be put to the annual general meeting.

By Order of the Board
The Lord Rayner, *Chairman*

London, 6 May 1987

All companies are required by the Companies Act, 1985, to file information on such things as the share capital and the names of Directors. This is done with the Registrar of Companies in Cardiff, as mentioned earlier. The file maintained for each company can be inspected by any member of the public.

Share capital

Ordinary shareholders have the right to vote at the Company's Annual General Meeting and they will receive a **dividend** on the shares that they hold, providing that the company is profitable. The exact amount or rate of dividend will depend very much on the performance of the business and normally not all of the profit will be distributed to shareholders. Some will be retained in the business for the benefit of future growth. **Corporation tax** is payable on profits earned by a company, the exact rate of which will be determined annually in the Chancellor of the Exchequer's Budget.

Preference shareholders do not usually have the right to vote at the Annual General Meeting and they receive a fixed rate of dividend which is paid before any dividend is paid to ordinary shareholders. In the event of a company going into **liquidation**, the preference shareholders have the right to the money they have invested to be returned after all the other claims on the assets on the company have been met. An ordinary shareholder only has the right to any money that may be left after all the creditors and preference shareholders have been paid. This could of course be nothing at all.

Preference shares are normally **cumulative**, meaning that if in any financial year there is insufficient profit to pay out dividends, the preference shareholders' right to the dividend is carried over to future years when the arrears of preference dividend have to be paid in full.

Activity 1

You have £500 to invest in the shares of a PLC. Look at the pages of a newspaper such as the *Financial Times*, where current share prices are quoted. Select shares in a company or companies of your choice and calculate the number of shares you can purchase with your £500.

At the end of four weeks look at the prices quoted in the Financial Press for the shares that you selected and calculate the value of the shares that you 'purchased'. You may continue this activity for any period. Some shares you have selected may have increased in value, others may have decreased. List the factors you think influence the current market price of a share and the reasons why share prices are subject to fluctuation.

Debentures

Unlike shares, a **debenture** is a loan which is made to a company. A company will raise money to finance the expansion of its operations by selling debentures. The debenture holder is paid interest on the amount loaned at a fixed rate of interest paid annually.

A debenture holder is in a completely different position to that of a shareholder. The debenture holder is not a member of the company and has no voting rights, but in the event of a company going into liquidation an **unsecured** debenture holder has the same rights as a creditor. A **secured** debenture holder's investment is protected in the event of liquidation because it is secured by a **charge** on a specific asset such as land or buildings. What this means is that proceeds of the sale of these assets must be paid to secured debenture holders to repay the sums of money that they have invested.

Activity 2

In Activity 3 in Block 1 you obtained the Annual Report and Financial Statements of a PLC of your choice. Examine the contents and consider the following questions:

a What is the authorized share capital?
b How many preference and ordinary shareholders are there?
c Has the PLC issued any debentures; if so, what is the annual interest rate?
d What was the dividend payable in the financial year to the ordinary shareholders?

Compare the sources of capital of the company you have selected with those of Marks and Spencer PLC as at 31st March 1987 which are reproduced on page 94.

Accounting Requirements for Limited Companies

The Directors and Managers of a Limited Company can draft accounts for **internal use** in any format they consider to be suitable to meet their needs. However, when it comes to publication, the Companies Acts dictate both the **information**

MARKS AND SPENCER p.l.c.

Providers of Group Capital

The capital of the Group arises from five sources:

1 Preference shares

The 1,350,000 preference shares are held by 841 shareholders, who receive dividends in preference to the holders of ordinary shares at rates of 7·0% and 4·9% per annum, plus related tax credit.

2 Ordinary shares

There are 270,581 holders of ordinary shares who receive dividends at rates declared either by the directors or at the annual general meeting. Their shareholdings are analysed as follows:

Size of shareholding	Number of shareholders	Percentage of total number of shareholders	Number of ordinary shares 000s	Percentage of ordinary shares
Over 1,000,000	263		1,396,435	52·6
500,001 – 1,000,000	191		138,128	5·2
200,001 – 500,000	328	0·8	106,221	4·0
100,001 – 200,000	448		65,717	2·5
50,001 – 100,000	1,033		73,645	2·8
20,001 – 50,000	4,747	1·8	144,227	5·4
10,001 – 20,000	11,647	4·3	163,394	6·2
5,001 – 10,000	28,355	10·5	201,161	7·6
2,001 – 5,000	67,505	25·0	221,646	8·3
1,001 – 2,000	59,726	22·1	92,751	3·5
501 – 1,000	44,783	16·5	35,703	1·3
1 – 500	51,555	19·0	14,657	0·6
	270,581	100·0	2,653,685	100·0

Those shareholders owning more than 100,000 ordinary shares are further analysed as follows:

Type of owner	Number of shareholders	Number of ordinary shares 000s
Insurance companies	108	434,129
Banks and nominee companies	529	743,094
Identifiable pension funds	102	262,702
Individuals	346	146,800
Others	145	119,776
	1,230	1,706,501

For the purposes of Capital Gains Tax the price of ordinary shares on 31 March 1982 was 153·50p each which, when adjusted for the 1 for 1 scrip issue in 1984, gives a figure of 76·75p each.

3 Debenture stocks

These stocks, with a nominal value of £45·0 million, are owned by Prudential Nominees Limited who are entitled to interest at annual rates ranging from 5·50% to 7·75% under the terms of the debenture trust deed.

4 8·25% Guaranteed Bonds 1996 (Eurobond)

US$150·0 million was raised this year by the issue of a Eurobond at an annual interest rate of 8·25% maturing in 1996. Currency and interest swaps were arranged to provide £100·0 millicn at floating interest rates below LIBOR.

5 Bank loans and overdrafts

Bank loans and overdrafts have been obtained to finance certain of the Company's subsidiaries and the overdrafts bear interest at rates varying with local bank rates.

that must be revealed and the **format** for its presentation in the various annual financial statements. Additional information also has to be shown in the form of **notes** to the main financial statements.

The Companies Act's accounting requirements can be split into three distinct areas:

1 **Books of account**—all companies are required to maintain **proper** books of account, in which records are kept of such things as the receipt and payment of cash, details of assets and liabilities, and details of suppliers and customers.
2 **Statutory books**—all companies are required to keep certain records, known as the statutory books, which include minute books of AGMs and meetings of Directors.
3 **Annual accounts**—It is the responsibility of the Directors to produce annually and deliver copies of the following to the Registrar of Companies:
   a Profit and Loss Account
   b Balance Sheet
   c Notes attached to *a* and *b* above
   d Directors' Report
   e The Auditor's Report

The Companies Acts detail the contents and format of the accounts and reports referred to above. In addition to the information that is specified in the Companies Acts, a PLC may if it wishes publish more detailed information.

Activity 3

List the Accounts and reports contained in the Annual Report and Financial Statements you obtained in Activity 2.

One of the reports you should have found is the Report of the Auditors. The Companies Act requires that a company should appoint an **Independent** Auditor at the AGM who will hold office from the conclusion of that meeting until the conclusion of the next AGM when the annual financial statements are presented.

The **External** Auditor of the company has therefore a **duty** to **report** to the **shareholders** on the financial statements produced by the directors. The External Auditor is appointed by the shareholders to protect their interests, and the audit that is carried out each year is to verify the accuracy of the accounts, which again relates to the concept of financial stewardship that is a function of being a director. The Auditor's Report must state whether, in the **Auditor's opinion**, the financial statements:

1 Have been properly prepared in accordance with the provisions of the Companies Acts.
2 Give a **true and fair** view of the financial state of affairs of the company for the financial year.

If the Auditor is **uncertain** about an item in the accounts, or if he **disagrees** with the treatment of a particular item in the accounts, then the Auditor's Report will be **qualified**.

The following pages contain extracts from the Annual Report and Financial Statement of Marks and Spencer PLC. You will see that the financial statements contain figures for the **Group** and the **Company**. The Group is composed of the Company, or **Parent Company**, and other companies or subsidiaries, including Marks and Spencer Companies in Canada, France, and the Netherlands.

Activity 4

a Look at the Profit and Loss Account of Marks and Spencer PLC (reproduced on page 99) and compare it with the Profit and Loss Account of S. Wing produced in Block 4.
b What was the total **turnover** of Marks and Spencer PLC in the financial year ended 31st March 1987?
c What do you think the expenses charged against profit were?
d What was the profit for the financial year?
e What does the undistributed surplus represent?

As we have seen in Block 4, the Trading and Profit and Loss Account is the basis for measuring the **performance** of a business in a financial year and it provides a basis for **comparison** with previous financial years. As you can see, in addition to the Consolidated Profit and Loss Account, Marks and Spencer PLC have published a pictorial summary of profits from 1983 to 1987.

There is strong competition among PLCs to produce published Annual Reports and Financial Statements that are innovative and interesting, yet meet the requirements of the Companies Acts for reporting purposes. The financial press and accounting journals are keen to comment on the presentation and content of PLCs' published Annual Reports and Financial Statements, with particular reference to the readability of the documents from the point of view of non-accountants.

MARKS AND SPENCER p.l.c.

Summary of Group Results

1987 Turnover (excluding sales taxes) £4,220·8m

1987 Profit: before tax £432·1m; after tax £276·0m

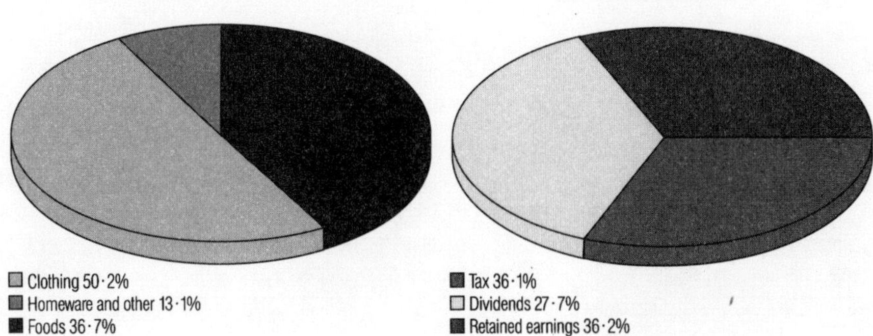

	% increase	1987 £m	1986 £m
Turnover (excluding sales taxes)	13·0	4,220·8	3,734·8
Clothing	13·5	2,118·4	1,866·0
Homeware	17·5	516·7	439·8
Foods	9·9	1,549·1	1,410·0
Financial activities	92·6	36·6	19·0
Profit on ordinary activities before tax	18·1	432·1	365·8
Profit for the financial year after tax	24·1	276·0	222·4
Earnings per share		10·4p	8·4p
Dividend per share		4·5p	3·9p
Dividend cover		2·3 times	2·2 times
Shareholders' funds		£1,579m	£1,452m
Ordinary shareholders' interests per share		59·44p	54·85p

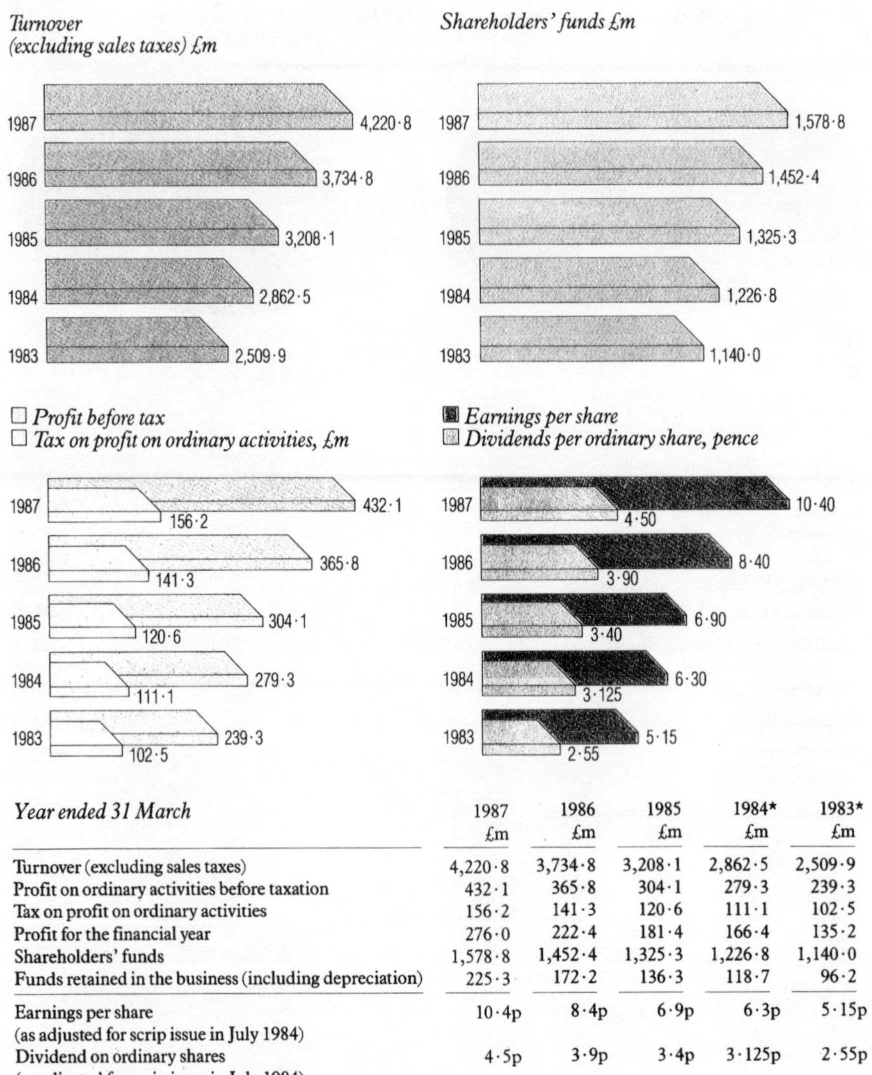

Year ended 31 March	1987 £m	1986 £m	1985 £m	1984* £m	1983* £m
Turnover (excluding sales taxes)	4,220·8	3,734·8	3,208·1	2,862·5	2,509·9
Profit on ordinary activities before taxation	432·1	365·8	304·1	279·3	239·3
Tax on profit on ordinary activities	156·2	141·3	120·6	111·1	102·5
Profit for the financial year	276·0	222·4	181·4	166·4	135·2
Shareholders' funds	1,578·8	1,452·4	1,325·3	1,226·8	1,140·0
Funds retained in the business (including depreciation)	225·3	172·2	136·3	118·7	96·2
Earnings per share (as adjusted for scrip issue in July 1984)	10·4p	8·4p	6·9p	6·3p	5·15p
Dividend on ordinary shares (as adjusted for scrip issue in July 1984)	4·5p	3·9p	3·4p	3·125p	2·55p

* Figures have not been restated to show translation using average rates of exchange.

MARKS AND SPENCER p.l.c.

Consolidated Profit and Loss Account

FOR THE YEAR ENDED 31 MARCH 1987

	Notes	1987 £m	1986 £m
Turnover	1	4,220·8	3,734·8
Cost of sales		2,915·8	2,666·5
Gross profit		1,305·0	1,068·3
Other expenses	2	872·9	702·5
Profit on ordinary activities before taxation	3	432·1	365·8
Tax on profit on ordinary activities	4	156·2	141·3
Profit on ordinary activities after taxation		275·9	224·5
Minority interests		(0·1)	2·1
Profit for the financial year	5	276·0	222·4
Dividends			
Preference shares		0·1	0·1
Ordinary shares:			
Interim of 1·4p per share		37·1	33·0
Final of 3·1p per share		82·3	70·1
		119·5	103·2
Undistributed surplus		156·5	119·2
Earnings per share	6	10·4p	8·4p

MARKS AND SPENCER p.l.c.

Balance Sheets

AT 31 MARCH 1987

	Notes	The Group 1987 £m	The Group 1986 £m	The Company 1987 £m	The Company 1986 £m
Fixed assets					
Tangible assets:	9				
Land and buildings		1,322·6	1,243·9	1,248·1	1,184·0
Fixtures, fittings and equipment		274·7	201·4	249·8	182·7
Assets in the course of construction		39·3	16·6	39·1	16·4
		1,636·6	1,461·9	1,537·0	1,383·1
Investments	10	—	—	154·9	67·5
Net assets of financial activities	11	51·3	18·3	—	—
		1,687·9	1,480·2	1,691·9	1,450·6
Current assets					
Stocks		255·4	235·3	206·5	197·7
Debtors	12	114·9	102·9	239·2	156·5
Investments	13	38·0	66·1	35·3	63·4
Cash at bank and in hand	14	58·8	106·2	21·0	19·4
		467·1	510·5	502·0	437·0
Current liabilities					
Creditors: amounts falling due within one year	15	529·9	481·7	469·6	422·0
Net current (liabilities)/assets (excluding financial activities)		(62·8)	28·8	32·4	15·0
Total assets less current liabilities		1,625·1	1,509·0	1,724·3	1,465·6
Creditors: amounts falling due after more than one year	16	46·3	46·1	145·0	45·0
Net assets		1,578·8	1,462·9	1,579·3	1,420·6
Capital and reserves					
Called up share capital	17	664·8	662·7	664·8	662·7
Share premium account		13·5	5·8	13·5	5·8
Revaluation reserve		86·4	84·0	86·7	86·7
Profit and loss account		814·1	699·9	814·3	665·4
Shareholders' funds	18	1,578·8	1,452·4	1,579·3	1,420·6
Minority interests		—	10·5	—	—
Total capital employed		1,578·8	1,462·9	1,579·3	1,420·6

Approved by the Board
6 May 1987

The Lord Rayner, *Chairman*

J K Oates, *Finance Director*

MARKS AND SPENCER p.l.c.

Consolidated Source and Application of Funds

FOR THE YEAR ENDED 31 MARCH 1987

	1987 £m	1986 £m
Cash and short-term funds at 1 April	136·7	101·1
Source of funds		
Arising from trading		
Profit on ordinary activities before taxation	432·1	365·8
Depreciation	67·8	52·7
Sales of fixed assets	4·5	5·5
	504·4	424·0
From other sources		
8·25% Guaranteed Bonds 1996 issue	100·0	—
Shares issued under employees' share schemes	9·8	6·9
	750·9	532·0
Application of funds		
Payment of dividends	107·3	94·3
Payment of taxation	137·3	119·7
Purchase of fixed assets	241·0	158·9
Acquisition of minority interest in Canadian subsidiary	53·5	—
Increase in inter-company funding of financial activities	100·0	—
Increase in net assets of financial activities excluding taxation (see below)	26·4	5·9
Miscellaneous	2·5	3·0
	668·0	381·8
Increase/(decrease) in working capital		
Stock	20·1	5·6
Debtors	14·9	47·5
Creditors under one year (excluding taxation and dividends)	(21·0)	(34·6)
Group relief payable to financial activities	2·6	(5·0)
	16·6	13·5
	684·6	395·3
Cash and short-term funds at 31 March	66·3	136·7

Cash and short-term funds comprise cash at bank and in hand and current asset investments less bank loans and overdrafts.

	1987 £m	1986 £m
Increase in net assets of financial activities		
Purchase of assets for finance leasing	2·5	0·1
Capital repayments on leases	(17·4)	(20·6)
Sale of leasing subsidiaries	(41·5)	—
	(56·4)	(20·5)
Purchase of fixed assets	6·2	4 3
Depreciation	(1·0)	(0·3)
Increase in trade debtors	60·9	84·2
Deferred tax eliminated on the sale of leasing subsidiaries	13·9	—
(Decrease)/increase in group relief receivable	(2·6)	5·0
(Increase) in bank loans, overdrafts and inter-company funding less cash	(9·7)	(75·1)
Increase in other working capital	15·1	8·3
Net movement	26·4	5·9

MARKS AND SPENCER p.l.c.

Accounting policies

Basis of accounting

The financial statements are drawn up on the historical cost basis of accounting, modified to include the valuation of the United Kingdom properties at 31 March 1982.

Basis of consolidation

The Group financial statements incorporate the financial statements of:
a The retailing activities of Marks and Spencer p.l.c. and its UK and European subsidiaries for the year to 31 March, and of the Canadian subsidiaries for the 14 months to 31 March (last year 12 months to 31 January 1986.)
b The financial activities of the Group's wholly-owned subsidiaries to 31 March. In order to reflect the different nature of the business of the financial activities and so present fairly the Group's state of affairs, the assets and liabilities of such activities are shown as a net investment in the Group balance sheet and are analysed separately in note 11 on pages 40 and 41.

Goodwill

Goodwill arising on consolidation which represents the excess of the consideration given over the fair value of the net tangible assets acquired is written off on acquisition against reserves.

Deferred taxation

Deferred taxation is provided on the liability method, to the extent that it is probable that a liability will crystallise. It is provided on the excess of capital allowances over depreciation in respect of assets leased to third parties and on certain items of income and expenditure included in the profit and loss account in different years from those in which they are assessed for taxation purposes.

Depreciation

Depreciation is provided to write off the cost or valuation of tangible fixed assets by equal annual instalments at the following rates:
Freehold and leasehold land over 99 years — Nil
Leasehold land 50-99 years — 1%
Freehold and leasehold buildings over 50 years — 1%
Leasehold land and buildings under 50 years — Over the remaining period of the lease
Fixtures, fittings and equipment — 10% or 20% according to the estimated life of the asset.

Foreign currencies

The trading results of overseas subsidiaries have been translated using average rates of exchange ruling during the financial year.

The balance sheets of overseas subsidiaries have been translated into sterling at the rates of exchange ruling at 31 March, except for those assets and liabilities where a forward exchange contract has been arranged, in which case this forward rate is used. Exchange differences arising between the translation into sterling of the net assets of these subsidiaries at rates ruling at the beginning and end of the year are dealt with through reserves.

The cost of the Company's investment in overseas subsidiaries is translated at the rate ruling at the date of investment. All other foreign currency assets and liabilities of the Company and its United Kingdom subsidiaries are translated into sterling at the rate ruling at 31 March, except in those instances where a forward exchange contract has been arranged in which case this forward rate is used. These exchange differences are dealt with through the profit and loss account.

Transactions during the year between the Company and its subsidiaries, customers and suppliers are translated into sterling at the rate of exchange ruling on the date of the transaction. All profits and losses on exchange realised during the year are dealt with through the profit and loss account.

Pension contributions

The Group operates pension schemes for the benefit of all its employees. The funds of the schemes are administered by Trustees and are separate from the Group. Independent actuaries complete valuations at least every three years and, in accordance with their recommendations, annual contributions are paid to the schemes so as to secure the benefits set out in the rules and the periodic augmentation of current pensions. The cost of these is charged against profits when the contributions arise.

Repairs and renewals

Expenditure on repairs, renewals and minor items of equipment is written off in the year in which it is incurred.

Stocks

Stocks which consist of goods for resale are valued at the lower of cost and net realisable value. Cost is computed by deducting the gross profit margin from the selling value of stock. When computing net realisable value an allowance is made for future markdowns.

Leases

For finance leases where the Group is the lessor, gross earnings are allocated to accounting periods such that the profit after tax represents a constant rate of return on the net cash investment in the lease during the period of the lease.

The net investment in finance leases which represents total lease payments receivable net of finance charges allocated to future periods, has been included under debtors in the net assets of financial activities.

Trading results in the United Kingdom

The trading results in the United Kingdom include transactions at stores up to and including the nearest Saturday to 31 March. All other transactions are included up to 31 March in each year.

MARKS AND SPENCER p.l.c.

Notes to the Financial Statements

1 Turnover

a Retailing
Turnover represents goods sold to customers outside the Group, less returns and sales taxes.

b Financial activities
Financial activities comprise the operation of the Marks and Spencer Chargecard together with leasing and insurance. Turnover represents the interest and other income attributable to these activities.

c Analysis of turnover — by activity and geographical market.

(i) Retailing	1987 £m	1986 £m
United Kingdom stores	3,809·1	3,395·4
Overseas stores:		
Europe	119·4	94·1
Canada (this year 14 months, last year 12 months)	210·7	181·5
	330·1	275·6
Export sales outside the Group:		
Europe	27·8	25·6
America	6·0	6·4
Africa	2·4	4·8
Far East	8·8	8·0
	45·0	44·8
	4,184·2	3,715·8
(ii) Financial activities	36·6	19·0
	4,220·8	3,734·8

Canadian turnover for the 12 months to 31 January 1987 was £188·5 million.

The turnover attributable to financial activities arises wholly within the United Kingdom and the Channel Islands.

9 Fixed assets — tangible assets

a The Group	Land and buildings					Assets	
					Fixtures, fittings &	in the course of	Total
		Long	Short		equip-	con-	fixed
	Freehold	leasehold	leasehold	Total	ment	struction	assets
	£m	£m	£m	£m	£m	£m	£m
Cost or valuation							
At 1 April 1986	791·8	430·7	65·0	1,287·5	319·9	16·6	1,624·0
Additions	23·3	18·0	6·9	48·2	127·1	65·7	241·0
Transfers from assets in the course of construction	17·2	21·6	4·2	43·0	—	(43·0)	—
Transfers from long to short leasehold	—	(1·4)	1·4	—	—	—	—
Disposals	(3·4)	(0·3)	(0·6)	(4·3)	(18·8)	—	(23·1)
Differences on exchange	3·5	1·1	(0·2)	4·4	2·1	—	6·5
At 31 March 1987	832·4	469·7	76·7	1,378·8	430·3	39·3	1,848·4
At valuation	614·4	346·5	12·6	973·5	—	—	973·5
At cost	218·0	123·2	64·1	405·3	430·3	39·3	874·9
	832·4	469·7	76·7	1,378·8	430·3	39·3	1,848·4
Accumulated depreciation							
At 1 April 1986	19·8	12·6	11·2	43·6	118·5	—	162·1
Depreciation for the year	5·5	3·5	4·5	13·5	54·3	—	67·8
Disposals	(0·3)	—	(0·6)	(0·9)	(17·7)	—	(18·6)
Differences on exchange	0·2	0·2	(0·4)	—	0·5	—	0·5
At 31 March 1987	25·2	16·3	14·7	56·2	155·6	—	211·8
Net book value							
At 31 March 1987	807·2	453·4	62·0	1,322·6	274·7	39·3	1,636·6
At 31 March 1986	772·0	418·1	53·8	1,243·9	201·4	16·6	1,461·9

MARKS AND SPENCER p.l.c.

Notes to the Financial Statements

CONTINUED

9 *Fixed assets — tangible assets* continued

b The Company	Land and buildings						
	Freehold £m	Long leasehold £m	Short leasehold £m	Total £m	Fixtures, fittings & equip-ment £m	Assets in the course of con-struction £m	Total fixed assets £m
Cost or valuation							
At 1 April 1986	756·2	419·8	40·0	1,216·0	282·1	16·4	1,514·5
Additions	22·9	9·5	1·2	33·6	117·8	65·7	217·1
Transfers from assets in the course of construction	17·2	21·6	4·2	43·0	—	(43·0)	—
Transfers from long to short leasehold	—	(1·4)	1·4	—	—	—	—
Disposals	(2·0)	(0·3)	(0·2)	(2·5)	(17·9)	—	(20·4)
At 31 March 1987	794·3	449·2	46·6	1,290·1	382·0	39·1	1,711·2
At valuation	614·4	346·5	12·6	973·5	—	—	973·5
At cost	179·9	102·7	34·0	316·6	382·0	39·1	737·7
	794·3	449·2	46·6	1,290·1	382·0	39·1	1,711·2
Accumulated depreciation							
At 1 April 1986	17·8	10·9	3·3	32·0	99·4	—	131·4
Depreciation for the year	5·2	3·2	1·9	10·3	49·8	—	60·1
Disposals	(0·1)	—	(0·2)	(0·3)	(17·0)	—	(17·3)
At 31 March 1987	22·9	14·1	5·0	42·0	132·2	—	174·2
Net book value							
At 31 March 1987	771·4	435·1	41·6	1,248·1	249·8	39·1	1,537·0
At 31 March 1986	738·4	408·9	36·7	1,184·0	182·7	16·4	1,383·1

(i) If the Company's land and buildings had not been valued at 31 March 1982 their net book value would have been:

	1987 £m	1986 £m
At valuation at 31 March 1975	362·3	362·3
At cost	548·8	473·7
At 31 March 1987	911·1	836·0
Accumulated depreciation	53·6	46·1
	857·5	789·9

The Company also valued its land and buildings in 1955 and in 1964. In the opinion of the directors unreasonable expense would be incurred in obtaining the original costs of the assets valued in those years and in 1975.

(ii) For fixtures, fittings and equipment detailed records of cost and depreciation are not maintained. The cost figures represent reasonable estimates of the sums involved.

10 Fixed assets — investments

a These investments comprise unlisted investments in and loans to subsidiaries.

	Shares in sub-sidiaries £m	Loans £m	Total £m
Cost			
At 1 April 1986	46·5	21·0	67·5
Additions	27·4	5·0	32·4
Redemptions	(1·4)	—	(1·4)
Canadian capital restructure	70·9	(14·5)	56·4
At 31 March 1987	143·4	11·5	154·9

b During the year the following major transactions affecting investments in subsidiaries took place:

(i) The Company subscribed for an additional 26·0 million £1 ordinary shares in St Michael Financial Services Ltd at a cost of £26.3 million.

(ii) The Company increased its holding in Marks and Spencer (Nederland) BV by acquiring shares for the following consideration:

(a) The C$35·0 million loan to Marks & Spencer Canada Inc. from Marks and Spencer p.l.c. was converted to share capital on 1 October 1986. These shares were transferred to Marks and Spencer (Nederland) BV.

(b) A payment of £53·5 million to fund the acquisition of the minority holding in Marks & Spencer Canada Inc.

(iii) The Company granted a subordinated loan of £5·0 million to St Michael Financial Services Ltd.

c The Company's principal subsidiaries are set out below. A schedule of interests in all subsidiaries is filed with the Annual Return.

	Principal activity	Country of incorporation and operation	Proportion of ordinary shares held by: The Company	A subsidiary
St Michael Financial Services Limited	Finance	England	100%	—
St Michael Finance Limited	Finance	England	100%	—
Marks and Spencer (Nederland) BV	Holding Company	The Netherlands	100%	—
Marks and Spencer Holdings Canada Inc	Holding Company	Canada	—	100%
Marks & Spencer Canada Inc.	Chain Store	Canada	—	100%
Marks and Spencer Finance (Nederland) BV	Finance	The Netherlands	—	100%
Marks and Spencer (France) SA	Chain Store	France	—	100%
Marks and Spencer (Ireland) Limited	Chain Store	Ireland	—	100%
SA Marks and Spencer (Belgium) NV	Chain Store	Belgium	—	100%
MS Insurance Limited	Insurance	Guernsey	—	100%
Baker Street Leasing Limited	Leasing	England	100%	—

The Company also owns all the participating preference shares in Marks and Spencer (Ireland) Limited.

MARKS AND SPENCER p.l.c.

Notes to the Financial Statements

CONTINUED

11 Net assets of financial activities	1987 £m	1986 £m
Fixed assets		
Land and buildings	0·5	0·4
Fixtures, fittings and equipment	3·7	3·3
Assets in the course of construction	5·0	0·3
	9·2	4·0
Current assets		
Debtors	186·2	184·5
Listed investments — market value £6·0 million (last year £5·1 million)	5·7	4·6
Cash at bank and in hand	25·3	2·2
	217·2	191·3
Current liabilities		
Creditors: amounts falling due within one year	67·6	145·0
Net current assets	149·6	46·3
Total assets less current liabilities	158·8	50·3
Creditors: amounts falling due after more than one year	100·1	5·0
Provisions for liabilities and charges:		
Deferred taxation	7·4	27·0
Net assets	51·3	18·3

a Fixed assets	Land & buildings Short leasehold £m	Fixtures, fittings & equip-ment £m	Assets in the course of con-struction £m	Total fixed assets £m
Cost				
At 1 April 1986	0·4	3·6	0·3	4·3
Additions	0·2	1·3	4·7	6·2
At 31 March 1987	0·6	4·9	5·0	10·5
Accumulated depreciation				
At 1 April 1986	—	0·3	—	0·3
Depreciation for the year	0·1	0·9	—	1·0
At 31 March 1987	0·1	1·2	—	1·3
Net book value				
At 31 March 1987	0·5	3·7	5·0	9·2
At 31 March 1986	0·4	3·3	0·3	4·0

Activity 5

Examine the Balance Sheets for Marks and Spencer PLC (on page 100) and then consider the following:

a The net book value of the fixed tangible assets of the group and company as at 31st March 1987 were £1,636.6 million and £1,537.0 million respectively. Look at the notes to the Financial Statements and calculate how these figures were arrived at.

b What is the amount of working capital for the company and the group as at 31st March 1987?

c What is (1) Called up Share Capital?
(2) Share Premium Account?
(3) Revaluation Reserve?

As we have seen, a Balance Sheet of a company shows the assets and liabilities as at the end of a financial year. By comparing the Balance Sheet with that produced at the end of the previous financial year, it is possible to calculate the changes in individual assets and liabilities that have taken place.

These changes are a result of the **flow of funds** in and out of the company during this accounting period. The Profit and Loss Account explains the majority of these changes as it details the profit earned during the financial year and the expenses that have been incurred. It also details amounts paid out from profit in the form of dividends and corporation tax.

A Source and Application of Funds Statement gives details of the flow of funds in a financial year as well as details of sources and applications of **working capital** in a financial year.

Activity 6

Look at the Consolidated Source and Application of Funds Statement for Marks and Spencer PLC on page 101.

a Why is depreciation a source of funds?

b Why is an increase in stock an increase in working capital?

c The total source of funds for 1987 was £750.9 million. How is the total application of funds figure arrived at?

Summary

This block has detailed the published accounts produced by public limited companies in order to comply with Companies Acts requirements. Public limited companies use their annual reports to publicize their business activities in addition to reporting on their financial performance during the year.

The next block examines the content and format of the published annual reports of local authorities. You will notice differences in the terminology used in the financial statements, but the basic concepts of accounting are no different.

Block 7 *Published Accounts of Public Sector Organizations*

Introduction

The previous block dealt with the published accounts of public limited companies. These companies exist to produce or sell products or provide a services, and range from retailing stores to banks.

Public sector organizations such as local government and health services also provide services, but not generally to make a profit. The services these organizations provide are usually taken for granted and include the provision of schools, colleges, doctors, and dentists. We all contribute to the provision of these services by paying taxes and rates (from 1990 the Community Charge).

Control needs to be applied within these public sector organizations to ensure that funds are properly used. This block looks at one area of the public sector in particular—local government—and examines how it operates and accounts for the money it spends in providing services. This block will help you to compare the accounts of a public limited company with those produced by a local authority.

This block is more like a case study in that it is concerned with one particular area of the public sector, and should provide a base for studies of central government accounting and health services accounting should you be interested in studying these areas.

The Structure of Local Government

The Local Government Acts of 1972 and 1985 contained the statutory provisions which established the present structure of local government in England and Wales.

These simple diagrams show how local government is administered and the relationships that exist between local and central government.

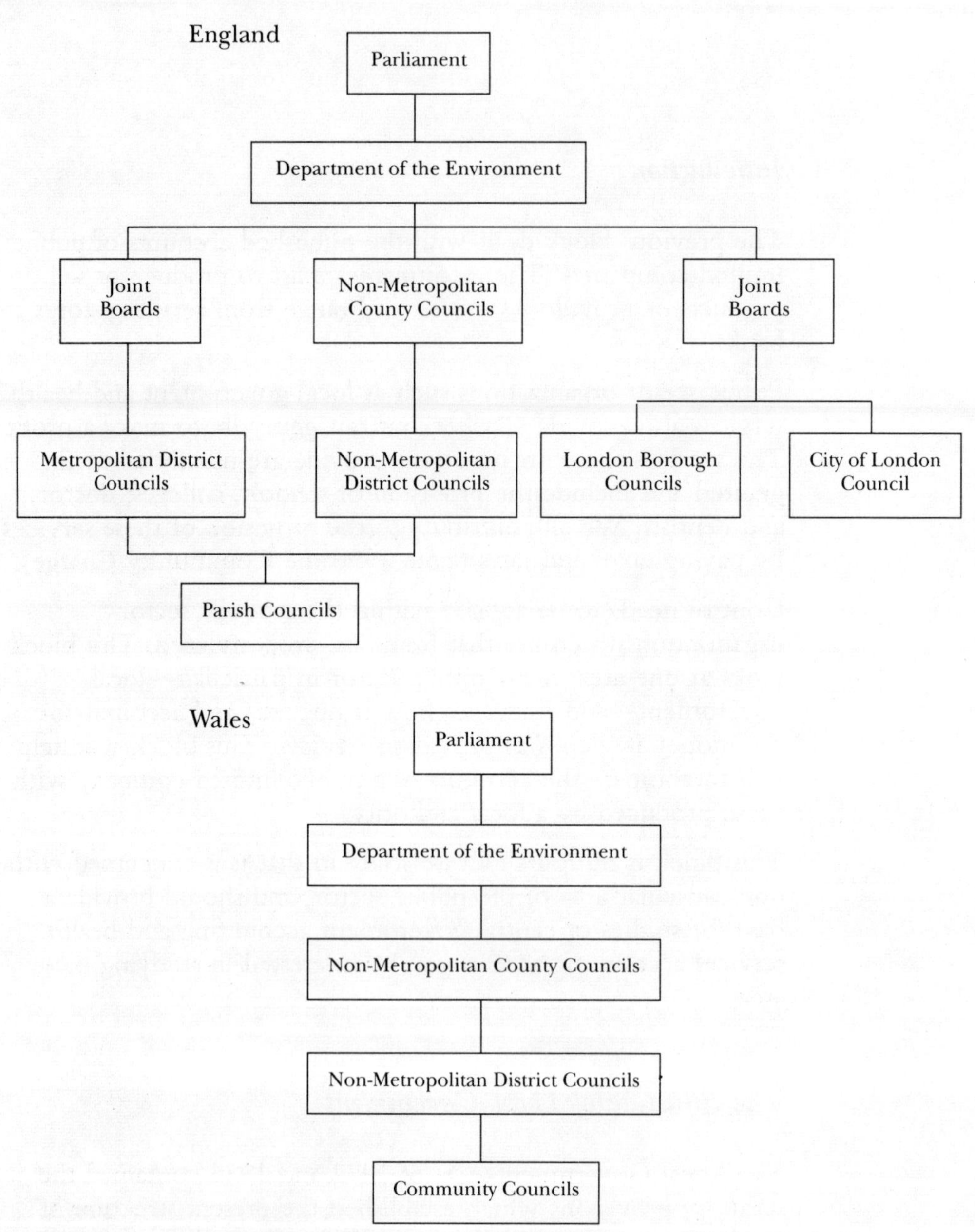

Local authority services are provided for the community and can be classified into the following groups:

Community Services
Protective Services
Personal Services
Trading Services

The elected members of a local authority, the councillors, determine service levels and priorities within the services provided and administered by a local authority in accordance with governmental and professional statutory guidelines, and with regard to the financial resources available. The role of the Chief Financial Officer and the finance staff of a local authority is to provide financial advice and accounting services which support this process as well as producing budgets and annual financial statements, for both internal use and external publication.

Activity 1

Obtain the latest annual report and accounts for a local authority in your area. Information will be provided in this report on the activities of the authority during a financial year—how many councillors sit on the council and which is the ruling political group? Classify the services of the local authority into the four groups listed above.

What is the population of the local authority's administrative area? Finally, how many people are employed by the authority and which service has the largest workforce?

Finance

In 1985/6, £35,231 million was spent by local authorities in the United Kingdom providing services to the community.

On average, 45% of the cost of running the services is paid for by Central Government in the form of grants. The other 55% is financed by means of a rate levied on the properties in the local authority's administrative area, the renting of council property, and charging for services such as the use of sports centres. Interest is also earned by investing surplus funds.

As local authorities were created by Acts of Parliament, as statutory corporations they can only carry out the functions for which they have a **statutory authority**.

This doctrine is open to interpretation, but it is generally accepted that a local authority must have a statutory authority for everything it does, either expressly given, or reasonably inferred, by an Act of Parliament. For example, the various Education Acts lay down the functions and duties of certain local authorities in relation to the provision of education. Local authorities therefore have a statutory duty to provide an education service. The policy makers within the authority interprete the statutory provisions and decide on the type of education system and the composition of the various schools in their area.

This statutory authority extends to the powers of local authorities to levy income and incur expenditure in relation to the discharge of their functions. If a local authority collects income or spends money for purposes for which it has no statutory authority then this income or expenditure can be deemed to be *ultra vires*, i.e. illegal and beyond the powers of the local authority. The failure to comply with a statutory duty to collect income is also illegal.

Under the arrangements for the annual external audit of local authorities contained in the Local Government Finance Act 1982, in addition to the external auditor's duty to certify that the annual financial accounts **present fairly** the financial transactions of the authority for that year, the auditor also has the duty to ensure that no item of account is unlawful or *ultra vires*. Where it appears to the auditor that any item of account is contrary to law, the auditor may apply to the court for a declaration that the item is unlawful. If the application is upheld, the court can order the person or persons responsible to repay the amount, and can also order rectification of the accounts.

In earlier blocks we looked at the distinction between **capital expenditure** and **revenue expenditure**. The same distinction applies when classifying expenditure for a local authority. Capital expenditure is on assets that have a life of more than one year; essentially expenditure on a fixed asset. Central Government controls the level of spending on capital items by local authorities by restricting the total capital payments made by each individual authority in a financial year. Under the provisions of the Local Government Planning and Land Act 1980, each local authority is given an annual capital payments allocation which can only be used for prescribed capital expenditure.

Revenue expenditure represents spending on day-to-day items such as the staffing and heat and light costs incurred in providing the services. In addition, instalments for repayment of loans and the payment of interest will also be classed as revenue expenditure.

Activity 2

Given this reminder of the distinction between capital and revenue expenditure, list any differences you think there might be in the items that appear under these headings for private companies and for local authorities.

Local authorities derive their revenue income from four distinct sources:

1 **The rate support grant**—this is paid to local authorities by Central Government to finance revenue spending, i.e. the costs of running services in a particular financial year. The Government determines the amount to be allocated each year through a system of **cash limits**. This means a ceiling is placed on the amount of money payable.

2 **Specific Government grants**—these are paid directly to local authorities by central government to finance certain services. The Home Office pays a 50% grant towards the provision of a police force, and similar grants are paid for housing improvement and student mandatory awards.

3 **Rates**—these are a form of local taxation levied on the occupiers and owners of property. The calculation of rates is based upon the property's rateable value, which is essentially a notional rent assessed by a valuer from the valuation branch of the Inland Revenue. Domestic rates will be replaced by the Community Charge from 1st April 1990.

4 **Rents, Charges, and Interest**—these include income from council house rents, charges for use of facilities, and interest earned from the investment of surplus funds.

The following pages give a pictorial summary of the revenue spending of Southampton City Council. Look through these charts and figures and then attempt the questions on page 118.

Pictorial Summary

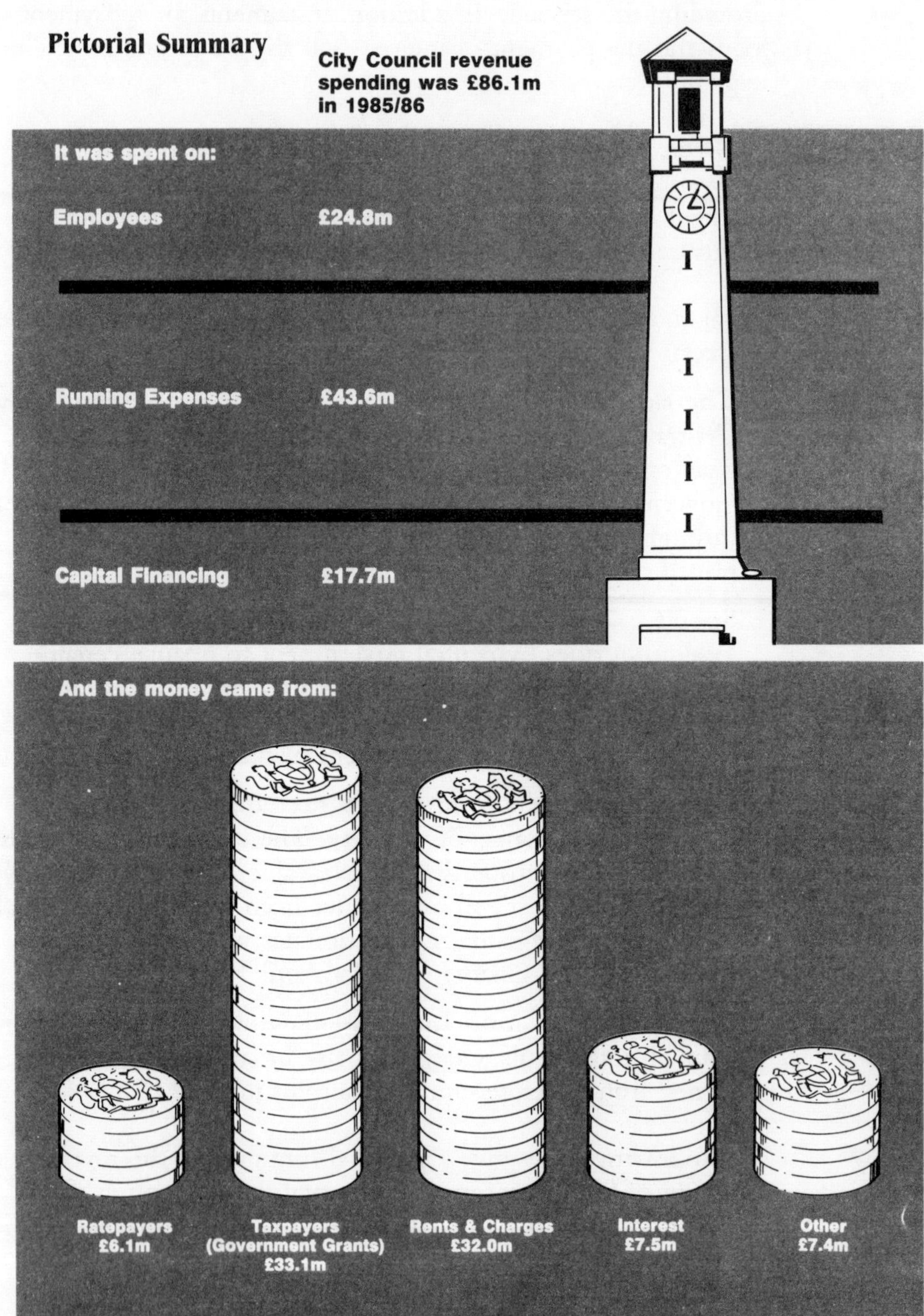

To provide:

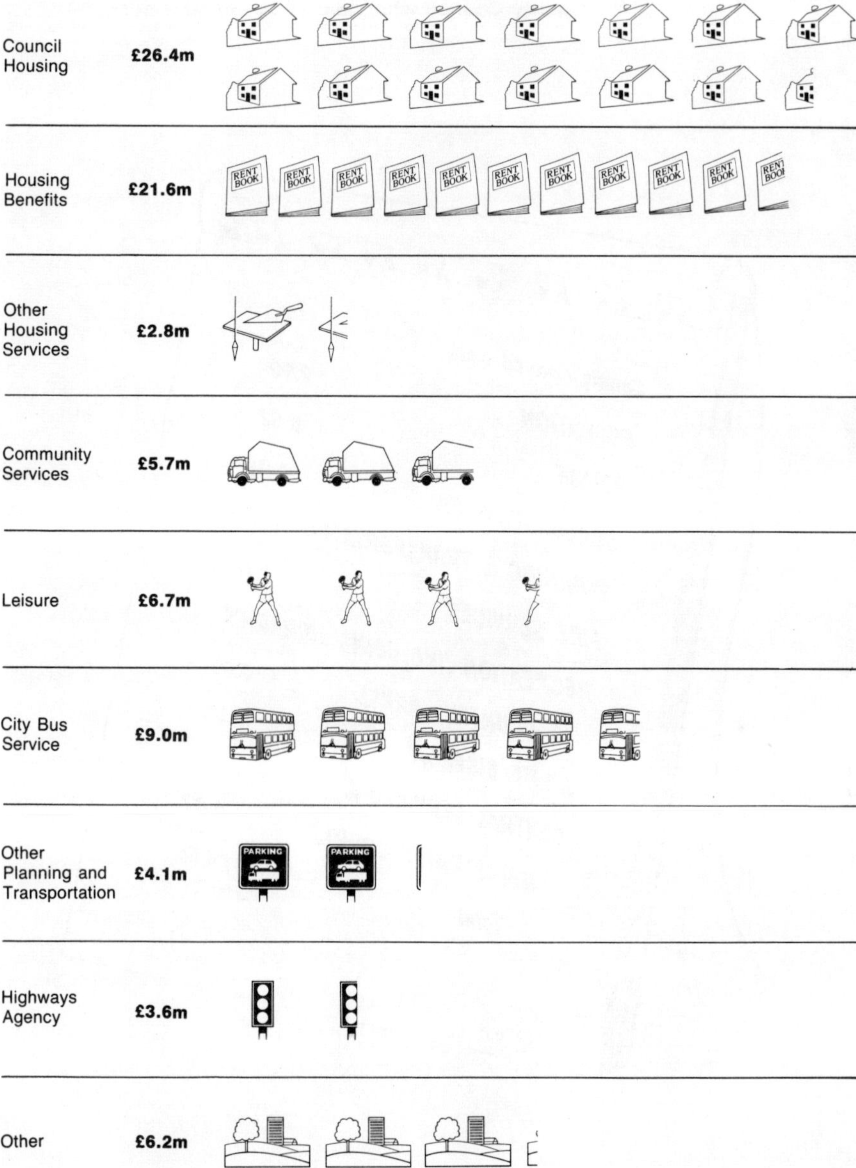
Council Housing
£26.4m
Housing Benefits
£21.6m
Other Housing Services
£2.8m
Community Services
£5.7m
Leisure
£6.7m
City Bus Service
£9.0m
Other Planning and Transportation
£4.1m
Highways Agency
£3.6m
Other
£6.2m

Pictorial Summary

In 1985/86 the typical domestic ratepayer paid £5.26 per week in rates. £4.55 was passed over to Hampshire County Council who planned to spend it on:

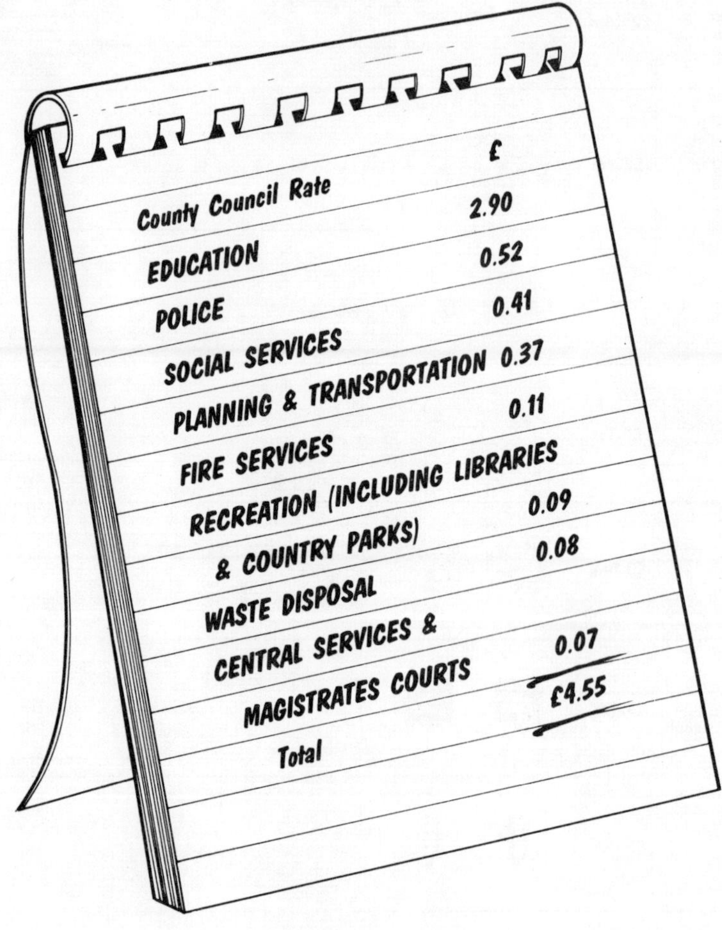

. . . . and the balance of 71 pence a week – about the cost of three pints of milk – was retained by Southampton City Council to provide:

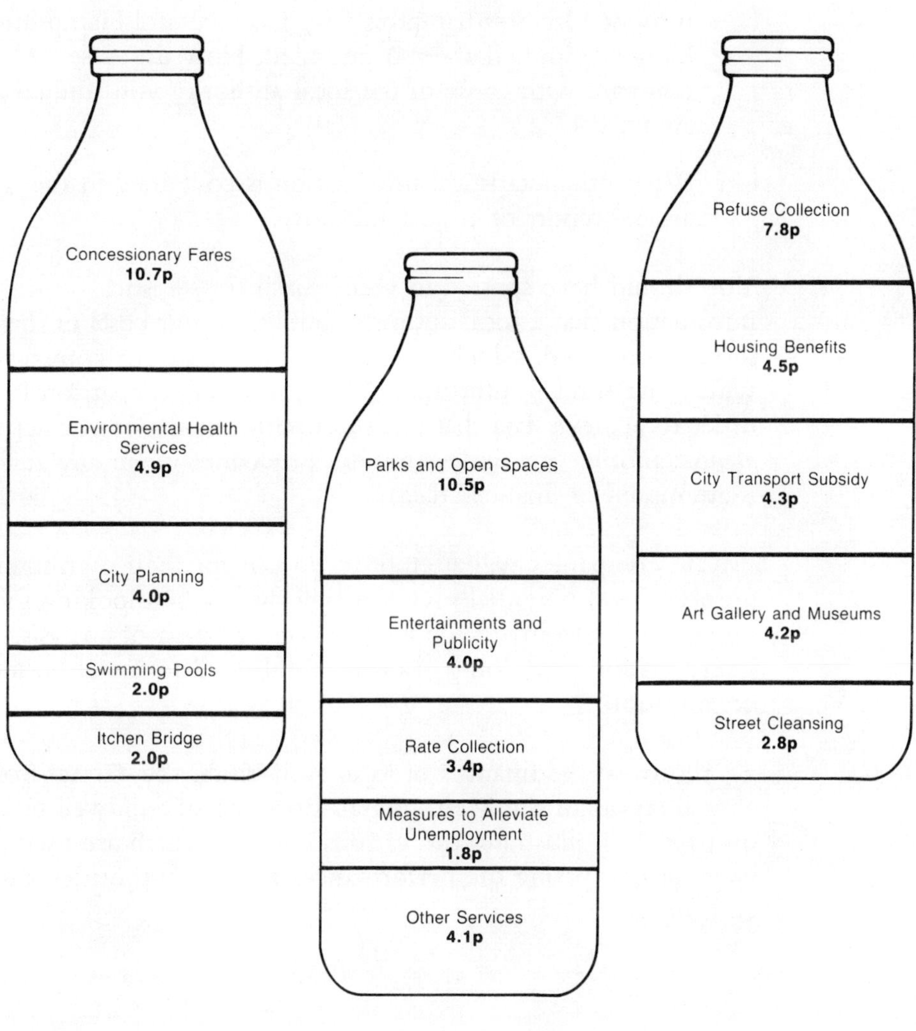

Activity 3

a What percentage of the total revenue spending is financed from

1 Government grants

2 Rates?

How do these percentages compare with those of the local authority you studied in Activity 1?

b Details of the costs of running the various services provided by Southampton City Council and Hampshire County Council are also provided. How do these compare with those of the local authority you studied in Activity 1?

c What other statistical information is contained in the annual report of a local authority?

You should have spotted in your search for statistical information that a local authority publishes unit costs of the services provided, which may be used as a basis for comparison with other similar authorities. This notion of comparison in order to achieve data that measures performance of one activity against another is a fairly common procedure when any analysis is attempted of financial data.

Private companies will attempt to do this for their own internal purposes, and potential investors will do it when looking for opportunities to invest funds. The concept then of analysis, interpretation, and comparison is useful in all forms of business organization.

To return to the finances of local authorities, the extract from annual report of the Metropolitan Borough of Sandwell given on page 119, illustrates the various statistics which are used as a basis for comparing the performances of local authorities with each other.

		Sandwell	Birm-ingham	Coventry	Dudley	Solihull	Walsall	Wolver-hampton	Average all MDC's
Population Reg. General Est. June 85		303,300	1,007,500	312,200	300,800	201,900	262,900	253,200	311,147
All Services									
Net Cost/1,000 Population	(£)	408,420	406,550	414,740	305,210	315,350	405,230	N/A	382,940
	(£)	(511,010)	(537,010)	(518,950)	(397,380)	(413,510)	(491,290)	(540,650)	(514,480)
Manpower/1,000 Population		32.05	31.26	N/A	23.38	19.97	31.28	36.87	31.96
		(53.02)	(51.92)	N/A	(42.61)	(38.85)	(57.19)	(62.46)	(N/A)
Education									
(1) **Primary & Nursery**									
Pupil Teacher Ratio		22.38	22.71	22.16	22.87	22.84	20.78	19.36	21.62
		(21.73)	(21.96)	(21.72)	(22.04)	(23.15)	(19.88)	(19.98)	(21.63)
Gross Cost per pupil	(£)	881	750	841	746	761	843	934	825
	(£)	(825)	(726)	(842)	(722)	(735)	(883)	(887)	(786)
(2) **Secondary**									
Pupil Teacher Ratio		14.85	16.32	15.18	14.91	16.14	14.59	14.73	15.51
		(14.55)	(15.34)	(13.98)	(15.42)	(16.22)	(13.40)	(15.01)	(15.29)
Gross Cost per pupil	(£)	1,269	1,188	1,330	1,180	1,138	1,220	1,272	1,204
	(£)	(1,301)	(1,167)	(1,279)	(1,128)	(1,099)	(1,329)	(1,251)	(1,200)
(3) **School Meals**									
Revenue/Cost Ratio	(%)	8.9	23.5	17.9	26.8	37.3	10.5	16.6	23.6
	(%)	(20.70)	(29.40)	(26.60)	(33.40)	(38.90)	(28.60)	(23.60)	(30.20)
Pupils receiving free school meals as a proportion of school roll	(%)	N/A	N/A	N/A	N/A	N/A	N/A	N/A	N/A
	(%)	(33.50)	(31.90)	(44.70)	(18.40)	(17.50)	(34.50)	(24.50)	(28.20)
(4) **Non-Advanced Further Education**									
Net Cost/1,000 Population	(£)	34.10	23.65	30.68	26.73	18.71	26.57	34.51	25.43
	(£)	(29,480)	(19,040)	(10,980)	(28,650)	(16,090)	(22,720)	(16,670)	(20,290)
(5) **All Education**									
Net Cost/1,000 Population	(£)	288,050	270,050	308,640	247,310	263,520	305,650	N/A	277,710
	(£)	(286,900)	(271,250)	(292,530)	(251,210)	(258,350)	(318,710)	(310,280)	(280,180)
Housing									
Rents paid as a percentage of total costs	(%)	34.80	27.80	19.80	39.00	36.70	31.70	N/A	34.50
	(%)	(36.80)	(30.40)	(20.40)	(36.90)	(38.30)	(32.40)	(35.30)	(33.20)
Management and maintenance costs per dwelling per week	(£)	7.08	6.81	11.02	8.52	6.37	N/A	N/A	6.27
	(£)	(5.02)	(8.12)	(9.04)	(8.65)	(7.50)	(7.62)	(9.23)	(6.54)
Social Services									
(1) **Children in Care**									
Children in Care as a proportion of population under 18	(%)	0.30	0.90	0.80	0.30	0.50	0.60	0.90	0.70
	(%)	(0.70)	(0.90)	(0.80)	(0.40)	(0.50)	(0.70)	(0.80)	(0.70)
Cost per child in residential care	(£)	14,611	10,903	19,601	18,398	20,287	15,108	17,745	14,211
	(£)	(10,606)	(12,101)	(23,720)	(15,748)	(13,988)	(13,126)	(13,853)	(14,362)
(2) **Care of Elderly**									
Supported Residents as a percentage of population aged 75+	(%)	3.81	3.12	3.16	2.92	2.98	3.90	3.92	3.52
	(%)	(N/A)	(N/A)	(N/A)	(N/A)	(N/A)	(N/A)	(N/A)	(N/A)
Cost per resident per week	(£)	110.32	123.39	133.70	116.41	99.98	101.24	127.15	116.46
	(£)	(113.04)	(129.25)	(131.51)	(110.49)	(96.94)	(106.01)	(145.21)	(117.78)
(3) **Fieldwork and Administration**									
Social Work Staff/1,000 Population		0.81	1.22	1.56	0.86	0.72	0.94	1.01	1.08
		(0.95)	(1.39)	(1.76)	(0.87)	(0.73)	(1.13)	(1.22)	(1.18)
(4) **Home Helps**									
Contact hours/1,000 Population aged 65+		15,356	11,754	16,130	13,547	11,103	10,960	17,781	16,637
		(15,246)	(16,347)	(15,538)	(12,938)	(12,683)	(11,718)	(19,441)	(17,539)
(5) **All Social Services**									
Net Cost/1,000 Population	(£)	50,550	60,810	73,490	37,980	39,770	45,560	65,590	57,760
	(£)	(58,210)	(72,310)	(76,500)	(40,890)	(42,420)	(55,600)	(75,710)	(64,710)
		Sandwell	Birm-ingham	Coventry	Dudley	Solihull	Walsall	Wolver-hampton	Average all MDC's
Recreation									
Net Cost/1,000 Population	(£)	17,900	19,900	11,100	10,900	8,000	11,000	N/A	16,200
	(£)	(16,950)	(19,030)	(10,260)	(11,050)	(7,370)	(10,760)	(11,150)	(16,840)
Libraries									
Total Cost/1,000 Population	(£)	6,540	10,130	6,500	7,790	8,230	7,520	7,630	8,000
	(£)	(6,630)	(10,710)	(7,240)	(8,230)	(8,810)	(7,790)	(8,260)	(8,320)
Staff/1,000 Population		0.51	0.67	0.47	0.44	0.45	0.54	0.55	0.59
		(0.53)	(0.70)	(0.45)	(0.44)	(0.46)	(0.55)	(0.58)	(0.59)
Refuse Collection									
Net Cost/1,000 Population	(£)	7,210	7,560	8,680	6,340	8,230	7,710	N/A	8,670
	(£)	(9,560)	(8,280)	(8,600)	(6,730)	(5,970)	(9,140)	(9,610)	(8,890)
Town and Country Planning									
(1) Net Cost/1,000 Population	(£)	5,280	10,626	4,724	4,978	N/A	4,303	4,610	6,108
	(£)	(9,172)	(14,506)	(7,239)	(5,488)	(N/A)	(5,815)	(9,779)	(7,613)
(2) Percentage of gross expenditure									
(i) Employees	(%)	17.9	14.0	30.2	42.9	N/A	32.4	N/A	24.2
	(%)	(20.8)	(14.9)	(27.0)	(45.8)	(N/A)	(38.8)	(14.4)	(25.2)
(ii) Central Administration Charges	(%)	11.9	11.4	17.3	22.3	N/A	30.7	N/A	13.5
	(%)	(9.7)	(10.6)	(10.6)	(20.6)	(N/A)	(27.5)	(25.3)	(12.2)
(iii) Capital Financing	(%)	56.0	65.3	34.7	32.0	N/A	6.7	42.3	47.8
	(%)	(55.2)	(53.8)	(36.8)	(31.0)	(N/A)	(7.3)	(44.5)	(43.9)

Activity 4

The following information relating to capital expenditure has been extracted from the Annual Report and Accounts of Southampton City Council for the Financial Year 1985/6.

Spending during the Year

	1985/86 Actual £'000	*Probable Outturn £'000*	*Variation 1985/86 £'000*
Major Projects			
Bitterne District Centre	65	95	(30)
Marlands	87	30	57
Crosshouse/Chapel Redevelopment	51	51	–
Upper Townhill Farm	4	60	(56)
St Mary Street	283	273	10
Gaumont/SCL	906	1,000	(94)
Woolston District Centre – Phase 1	170	202	(32)
Mayfield Park Changing Accommodation	133	129	4
Town Depot Redevelopment – Phase 1	110	148	(38)
Eastpoint	84	156	(72)
Local Projects	58	100	(42)
Other Schemes	35	96	(61)
Total Major Projects	**1,986**	**2,340**	**(354)**
Housing			
Housing Revenue Account	13,919	11,393	2,526
Housing – GRF Services	2,601	2,777	(176)
Housing Act Advances	70	106	(36)
Total Housing	**16,590**	**14,276**	**2,314**
Geothermal Energy	**11**	**–**	**11**
Other Projects			
Policy & Resources	249	396	(147)
Community Services	42	50	(8)
Leisure	287	355	(68)
Planning & Transportation	363	888	(525)
Transport Undertaking	618	636	(18)
Total Other Projects	**1,559**	**2,325**	**(766)**
	20,146	**18,941**	**1,205**

Source	*£'000*
Capital Receipts	8,532
Loans	7,755
Capital Fund	1,637
Revenue Reserve for Capital Purposes	1,204
Other	1,018
	20,146

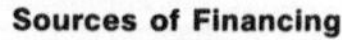

Sources of Financing

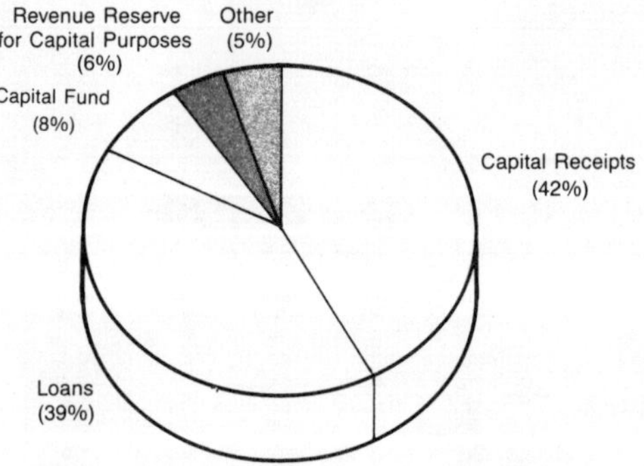

As you can see, the capital expenditure on the purchase of fixed assets has been financed from other sources in addition to the raising of loans.

a What are these other sources of capital finance?

b What methods of financing capital expenditure were used by the local authority you studied in Activity 1?

c List all the sources of financing capital expenditure that can be used by a local authority. How do these compare with sources available to public limited companies?

There is an obligation on all local authorities and their Chief Financial Officers to adopt proper accounting practices and make full disclosure of all relevant financial information within the published Statement of Accounts. The Local Government Act 1972 details the responsibilities of officers and the obligations of local authorities with regard to the detail that has to be provided in accounting statements. Essentially this act, and others that have followed, provides a legal framework for the style of reporting and a regulatory framework to safeguard the interests of ratepayers and others who provide income.

The majority of Chief Financial Officers and accountants employed in local authorities are members of the Chartered Institute of Public Finance and Accountancy (CIPFA). As such, the professional obligations of accountants are controlled, and all officers must adhere to the standards and guidelines that are issued. These include Statements of Standard Accounting Practice, and therefore the framework of regulations is essentially very similar to that governing public companies. An additional control on local authorities comes from the Audit Commission which requires that the Auditor appointed be satisfied that the accounts have been prepared in accordance with specific CIPFA guidance and with good practice.

Activity 5

List all the financial statements contained in the Annual Report and Accounts that you obtained in Activity 1, for a local authority in your area. Compare the statements with those contained in the annual report of a public limited company.

The financial statements produced by the local authority are:

1 General Rate Fund Revenue Account
2 A Consolidated Balance Sheet
3 A Consolidated Source and Application of Funds Statement

In comparing these statements with those produced by a Public Limited Company you will notice that a local authority does not produce a Profit and Loss Account.

In addition to the accounts listed above there is a requirement to publish Revenue Accounts for individual services.

When the balance sheets of all individual services are complete, they will be put together in the form of a consolidated balance sheet for the local authority as a whole.

The following extracts are from the accounts relating to the Housing Revenue Account published in the annual report for 1985/6 of Southampton City Council.

Housing Revenue Account

Revenue Summary

1984/85 Actual £'000		Employees £'000	Running Expenses £'000	Capital Financing £'000	Total £'000	Probable Outturn £'000	Variation £'000
	Expenditure						
	Premises –						
6,742	Repairs	363	7,218	–	7,581	7,153	428
17	Rent Payable	–	20	–	20	21	(1)
–	Maintenance Allowance	–	317	–	317	325	(8)
	Supervision & Management –						
67	Debt Management	–	–	62	62	66	(4)
1,875	Management (General)	1,050	1,192	–	2,242	2,335	(93)
3,389	Management (Special)	675	3,019	–	3,694	3,739	(45)
10,991	Capital Financing	–	–	12,626	12,626	12,587	39
23,081	**Total Expenditure**	**2,088**	**11,766**	**12,688**	**26,542**	**26,226**	**316**
	Income						
	Rent income from –						
16,246	Dwellings				17,067	17,058	9
680	Garages, Shops, etc.				696	694	2
16,926	Total Rents				17,763	17,752	11
1,541	Heating Charges				1,613	1,610	3
4,876	Interest Received				6,239	6,240	(1)
131	Voluntary GRF Contribution				163	158	5
–	Housing Defects Act Subsidy				24	8	16
21	Miscellaneous				20	19	1
23,495	**Total Income**				**25,822**	**25,787**	**35**
414	Surplus/(Deficit) For Year				(720)	(439)	(281)
	Balances						
1,513	Balance Brought Forward				1,927	1,927	–
414	Surplus/(Deficit) for Year				(720)	(439)	(281)
1,927	**Balance Carried Forward**				**1,207**	**1,488**	**(281)**

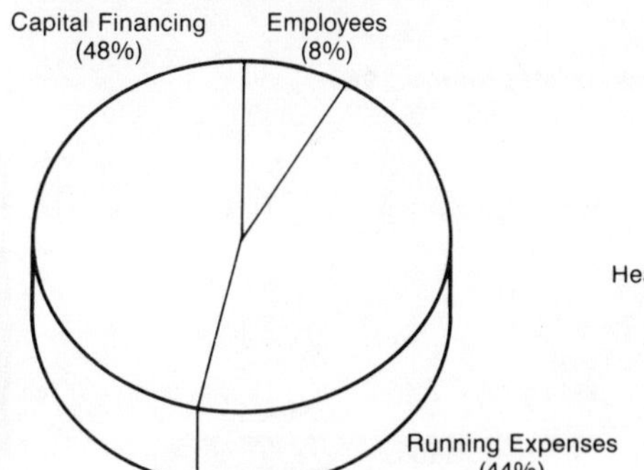

Make up of Income

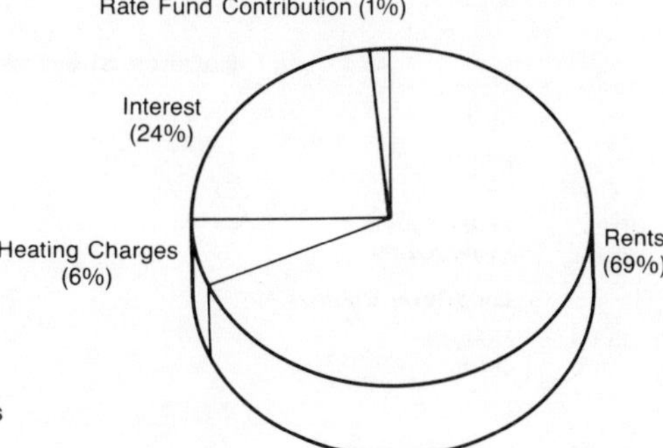

Capital Expenditure

Service	*Actual*	*1985/86 Probable Outturn*	*Variation*
	£'000	*£'000*	*£'000*
Dwelling Construction	5,668	1,825	3,843
Council House Modernisation	4,552	4,003	549
Housing Defects Act	1,386	1,700	(314)
Capitalised Repairs	1,063	1,633	(570)
Do It Yourself Shared Ownership	764	750	14
Other Dwelling Improvements	196	135	61
Environmental Improvements	121	784	(663)
Land Acquisition	77	500	(423)
Site Development	45	3	42
Acquisition Of Existing Dwelling	25	25	–
Acquired Dwellings Improvement/Repairs	11	24	(13)
Furniture For Old People's Homes	11	11	–
	13,919	**11,393**	**2,526**

Type of Expenditure	*1985/86*
	£'000
Purchase of Land and Buildings	2,254
Works	10,821
Fees and Salaries	395
Plant and Equipment	259
Loans and Grants	190
	13,919

Statistics

1984/85		*1985/86*
21,910	Number of dwellings at 31st March	21,544
363	Number of sales	451
63	Number of new completions	92
329	Number of dwellings modernised	409
2.5%	Rent arrears (as % of gross annual debit)	2.3%
1.3%	Vacant properties % of stock	2.5%
0.8%	Vacant properties % of lettable stock	1.3%
3.1%	Vacant properties in private sector in Southampton	2.9%

Housing Revenue Account

Balance Sheet as at 31st March 1986

1985 £'000		£'000	£'000	£'000	Notes (See pages 63 to 68)
91,953	**Fixed Assets**		97,076		**4**
25,211	**Investments**		27,446		**6**
	Long Term Debtors				
19,314	Mortgages	17,233			**7**
870	Other	852			**8**
20,184			18,085		
27	Deferred Charges		26		
137,375	**Non Current Assets**			**142,633**	**9**
	Current Assets				
1,074	Debtors	1,485			**11(a)**
293	Cash at Bank	38			
1	Cash in Hand	1			
1,368			1,524		
	Current Liabilities				
(1,484)	Creditors	(1,659)			**11(b)**
(4,350)	Temporary Borrowing	(6,060)			
(5,834)			(7,719)		
(4,466)	**Net Current Assets**			**(6,195)**	**17**
132,909				**136,438**	
	Financed By:				
91,998	Long term borrowing			97,118	**15**
38,947	Reserves			37,799	**18**
37	Provisions			314	
1,927	Revenue Account Balance			1,207	**20**
132,909				**136,438**	

The Revenue Account is the equivalent of the Trading and Profit and Loss Account published by a public limited company. The terms 'Profit and Loss' are replaced by the terms 'Surplus and Deficit'.

Other features that are different include the fact that there is no charge for depreciation in the annual accounts of local authorities. Because the normal method of financing the purchase of a fixed asset is by raising a loan, the repayment period of the loan broadly relates to the life of the asset and so the annual loan repayments are charged to the Revenue Account. This can be seen as the equivalent of depreciation which appears in the accounts of public limited companies.

There is strong competition between local authorities to achieve the most readable and understandable Annual Report and Accounts. The CIPFA makes an annual award to the local authority that is judged to produce the 'best annual report'. This has the effect of stimulating constant changes in the way these reports are produced.

Activity 6

Having looked now at some of the reports of local authorities and also, we hope, collected some published accounts of public companies, attempt some comparison by looking, not just at the factual information produced, but also at the 'cosmetic' appearance of the reports. Do you think there is evidence of these organizations being aware of the image that is being created and therefore the potential of the documents as some form of advertisement for the company or local authority?

Summary

This block has examined the annual report of a local authority, other public sector organizations, such as central government departments, and health authorities which also produce detailed annual reports containing financial statements.

Regardless of the type of organization and its function, the basic objective of the annual report and financial statements is to present the activities of the organization in a form that the reader can read and understand. This theme continues in the next block which looks at performance analysis.

Block 8
Performance Analysis

Previous blocks have introduced the concept of financial measurement, and looked at ways in which firms can assess their performance. We will now look further at the assessment of a business in terms of its success in two main areas:
1 Profitability
2 Liquidity.

Firms need to generate not only profit, but also **liquid resources** so that they remain solvent. Measuring profits is a fundamental feature of any accounting system, and the recording of the profit in the Profit and Loss Account is an expected and necessary facet of the recording system and accounting function. However, measuring profit or any other 'absolute' does not give any indication of the effectiveness and efficiency of the organization. Relationships help to give a better idea of the performance of any activity by expressing ratios that exist between two features.

In simple terms this means measuring profit in terms of resources used up to achieve the profit.

All accounting statements need to be interpreted if the reader or user is to be able to assess the performance of the organization. Profit and Loss Accounts and Balance Sheets as simple statements are effective in reporting data, but not effective as measuring instruments without some degree of analysis and interpretation. Interpretation can involve comparison—either with budgets or with previous periods, or perhaps with a similar firm operating in a similar line of business.

We will look at the Trading and Profit and Loss Account and Balance Sheet of two companies, both engaged primarily as retailers.

Saleways Company
Trading and Profit and Loss Account for year ended 31st December 19X9

	19X8	19X9
	£	£
Sales	650,000	610,000
Opening stock	24,400	31,300
add Purchases	492,000	438,000
	516,400	469,300
less Closing stock	31,300	26,400
Cost of goods sold	485,100	442,900
Gross profit	164,900	167,100
less Wages	123,900	124,700
Travelling expenses	1,800	2,100
Electricity	530	920
Rates	650	790
	126,880	128,510
Net Profit	38,020	38,590

Balance Sheet as at 31st December 19X9

	19X8	19X9
	£	£
Fixed Assets		
Buildings and fixtures	280,000	280,000
Vehicles	23,000	20,000
	303,000	300,000
Current Assets		
Stock	31,300	26,400
Debtors	2,700	2,020
Cash	400	580
	34,400	29,000
Current Liabilities		
Creditors	6,700	6,200
Tax owing	3,000	3,100
Bank overdraft	2,300	4,700
	12,000	14,000
Net Current Assets	22,400	15,000
	325,400	315,000
Financed by		
Capital	250,000	260,000
Mortgage loan	75,400	55,000
	325,400	315,000

Greengate Company
Trading and Profit and Loss Account for Year Ended 31st December 19X9

	19X8	19X9
	£	£
Sales	296,000	338,000
Opening Stock	19,400	27,300
add Purchases	218,000	242,000
	237,400	269,300
less Closing Stock	27,300	22,300
Cost of goods sold	210,100	247,000
Gross Profits	85,900	91,000
less Wages	44,300	45,600
Rents and rates	1,900	2,100
Electricity	2,730	2,900
Interest	1,690	1,700
	50,620	52,300
Net Profit	35,280	38,700

Balance Sheet as at 31st December 19X9

	19X8		19X9	
	£		£	
Fixed Assets				
Fixtures & fittings	52,100		56,300	
Vehicles	49,800	101,900	46,200	102,500
Current Assets				
Stock	27,300		22,300	
Debtors	9,500		10,200	
	13,800		21,100	
	50,600		53,600	
Less				
Current Liabilities				
Creditors	14,200		13,800	
Tax owing	6,500		3,900	
Bank overdraft	2,200		–	
	22,900		17,700	
Net Current Assets		27,700		35,900
		129,600		138,400
Financed by				
Capital				
Loan—6 years duration		91,600		100,400
Repayable 1 year after 19X9		38,000		38,000
		129,600		138,400

Because the documents have comparative figures it is possible to draw certain conclusions from a simple comparison of the results of the two years. However, to measure more significant features, ratios can be produced by the following methods.

Profitability Measures

Net Profit as Percentage of Capital employed $= \dfrac{\text{Net Profit}}{\text{Capital employed}} \times \dfrac{100}{1}$

For Saleways 19X9 $\dfrac{£38,590}{£315,000} \times \dfrac{100}{1} = 12.25\%$

Net Profit as Percentage of Sales $\dfrac{£38,590}{£610,000} \times \dfrac{100}{1} = 6.33\%$

Sales : Capital Employed £610,000 : 315,000 = 1.94%

These ratios can be displayed in the form of a 'Pyramid of Ratios' thus:

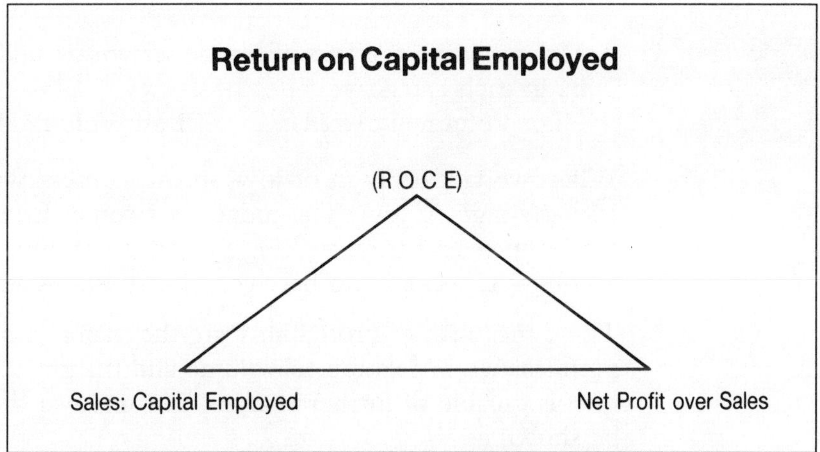

Putting the figures for Saleways into the pyramid we get:

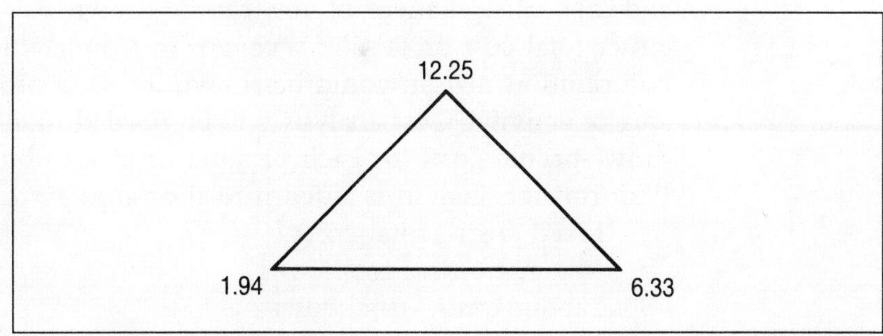

We can see that the top of the return on capital employed pyramid (shown on page 129) is made up of the two relationships shown in the bottom two points.

$$1.94 \times 6.33 = 12.25$$

Therefore we can use this set of relationships to illustrate that a business generating a return on its capital of 12.25% has done so by achieving on average a profit of 6.33% on each sale made and then generating a volume of sales at this average percentage sufficient to give a return of 12.25% on the capital utilized in the business. In this instance the volume or quantity of sale represents 1.94 times the amount of capital that is employed in the business. In other words the capital employed has 'turned over' 1.94 times, and this reveals to interested parties a feature or style of trading.

What these ratios do is to display the features of a business that contribute to its success or failure, and managers in business will need to know in detail how these ratios or relationships were derived. A certain style of trading is usually revealed, perhaps high volume–low margin or low volume–high margin.

Activity 1

Make a list of the sort of businesses you would expect to be in each category

High Volume–Low Margin   Low Volume–High Margin

When we talk of 'high or low' in this context we mean *relatively* high or low. The judgement comes from knowledge of the business and from making meaningful comparisons between accounting periods and between your business and others.

These measures of profitability are the major indications of performance in relation to volume and margin. Each of these in turn is capable of further analysis. For instance the margin can be shown as

$$\frac{\text{Gross Profit}}{\text{Sales}}$$

and then each element of cost can be shown as a percentage of either total cost or of sales revenue. In manufacturing firms, the contribution margin could be shown for each product line or area of activity. Cost analysis will be needed in all businesses to show specific costs for each product or area of business. Performance analysis is aided if relationships are calculated for:

Fixed costs : total costs
Material costs : total costs
Labour costs : total costs

Alternatively, each cost can be shown as a percentage of sales value. The important point is that any relationship that is meaningful should be calculated as one total ratio, (for example, profit to capital employed can be seen as the ultimate device to measure achievement), but which is both capable and in need of subdivision so that managers and other interpreters can assess the factors that have contributed to this major ratio.

There are many ratios that can be grouped under the general heading of operating efficiency ratios, and are intended to give information about specific areas within a business. Major areas include:

1 *Stock Turnover*

This is calculated by expressing the cost of goods sold over the average stock held. As a general rule, the higher the rate of stock turnover the better, as this indicates that capital invested in stock is capable of being repaid quickly because stock is sold and will generate cash back into the business.

2 *Number of Days Outstanding in Debtors*

Control over debtors is important as this impinges on the areas of liquidity. The quicker money comes in the better, therefore a careful monitoring exercise needs to be carried out over debtors. Often the 'number of sales days' outstanding in debtors is calculated by showing the relationship between debtors and sales and multiplying by 365.

We are now looking at areas that affect not just profitability but liquidity in a business. At the beginning of this block we said that performance control needs to be exercised over profitability and liquidity, and the ratios that are conventionally calculated to measure liquidity are taken from the Balance Sheet.

The working capital part of the Balance Sheet is the section that reveals some information about liquidity. The relationship between current assets and current liabilities, for instance, is a general measure of the ability to pay current debts as they fall due. This is a very general measure and the problem with using this as a single indicator of performance is that the Balance Sheet itself, from which the figures are taken, is limited by the very concepts and conventions that govern its production. The Balance Sheet is sometimes called a 'Position Statement' because the figures given to show assets owned and liabilities outstanding are correct only at Balance Sheet date—usually the last day of the accounting period. If we are attempting to measure liquidity, then taking figures from the Balance Sheet will indicate it at balance sheet date only, and by definition liquidity is required constantly throughout the year.

This limitation will in fact apply to any judgements made by taking values from a Balance Sheet. To dwell on liquidity features, however, we must appreciate that constant movement will be taking place as goods are received and sold; cash is both paid out and received, and contracts are being entered into for both purchases and sales. It is possible that there has been either a large increase or decrease in stocks immediately prior to the Balance Sheet date. Similarly debtors may pay the day after Balance Sheet date, confounding any simple conclusions drawn from ratios calculated by using figures true at the last day of the accounting period but not necessarily true at any other date.

Nevertheless, a systematic presentation of ratios comparing relationships over different accounting periods can be extremely useful. Normal ratios calculated will include:

1 Current assets : current liabilities
2 The acid test ratio—the assets that are more immediately convertable to cash are compared to the liabilities that are likely to be current.

The difficulty is in knowing which of the current assets can be sensibly deemed to be quickly convertable into cash. Is it debtors? The answer depends on credit control policies and the nature of the business's style of trading. Is it stock? The answer again depends on whether the business is a retail organization selling stock quickly for cash, or one involved in manufacturing where the time lag between converting stock into products and receiving cash from customers buying those products can be extensive.

Activity 2

List the sorts of ratios that you think would be useful in
a Manufacturing businesses, and
b Retail organizations.

Activity 3

The following information has been extracted from the published accounts of a major manufacturing company.

	1985	1986	1987
Return on capital employed	10%	21.6%	24.2%
Profit margin on sales	5.3%	9.4%	11.5%
Capital turnover	1.9	2.3	2.1

Discuss how the performance of the business has changed and suggest what might have happened over the three years to cause the changes outlined in the statistics above.

Activity 4

(This activity is also found in *Finance*.)
A friend of yours is thinking of investing in one of two manufacturing companies. Summarized accounts for the two companies are shown below.

Write your advice to your friend, outlining with sound financial reasoning which company you would choose and the advantages and disadvantages of each one.

Balance Sheet at 30 September 19X8

	Factors and Co.		Makit and Co.	
	£000	*£000*	*£000*	*£000*
Freehold property at revaluation 1988		9,800		—
Plant, machinery, and equipment at cost	8,400		11,200	
depreciation	7,700	700	2,800	8,400
Goodwill		—		4,200
Stocks: finished goods		1,400		700
work in progress		2,800		1,400
Debtors		6,300		2,800
Bank deposit		—		4,200
		21,000		21,700
less Creditors	6,300		4,900	
Overdraft	2,100	8,400	—	4,900
		12,600		16,800
Capital		9,100	—	10,500
Loans		3,500		6,300
		12,600		16,800
Additional information				
Sales		14,000		14,000
Net profit		2,800		3,500

Activity 5

A local business is operated by a trader as a 'one-man' business or sole trader.

Compare the performance for the past two years by calculating ratios. Explain what has happened to the business over the two-year period.

		Year 1		Year 2
		£		£
Opening stock		—		10,000
Purchases		80,000		119,500
Closing stock		10,000		15,500
Sales		100,000		150,000
Gross profit		30,000		36,000
Operating expenses		18,000		20,000
Net profit		12,000		16,000
Balance sheet information				
Fixed assets		11,000		10,000
Working capital				
Stock	10,000		15,500	
Debtors	8,000		13,500	
Cash	2,000	20,000	—	29,000
Creditors		7,000		11,000
Bank		—		2,000
		13,000		16,000
Capital		24,000		24,000
Add Net profit		12,000		16,000
		36,000		40,000
Less Drawings		12,000		14,000
		24,000		26,000

Activity 6

Prepare relevant ratios from the following balance sheets:

Fixed Assets	£000	£000	£000	£000
Land and Buildings		7,700		7,700
Plant and Machinery		780		600
Vehicles		140		110
Fixtures, Fittings, and Equipment		90		75
		8,710		8,485
Current Stocks				
Stocks	355		310	
Debtors	63		57	
Cash at Bank and in Hand	134		180	
	552		547	

	£000	£000	£000	£000
Current Liabilities				
Creditors	230		290	
		322		257
		9,032		8,742
Capital Reserves				
Authorized, Issued & Fully Paid,				
8 million ordinary shares of £1 each		8,000		8,000
Profit & loss account		1,032		742
		9,032		8,742
Extract From Profit & Loss Accounts				
Sales		7,675		7,022
Net profit		1,635		1,299

The activities in this block, indeed in most of the blocks, require you to put yourself in the position of either a presenter or user of accounting data. 'Users' are generally perceived as being managers, owners, potential shareholders, or the Inland Revenue. There are of course other interested parties like Trades Unions, employees, and creditors, who may look for different information for different purposes.

Activity 7

List the potential users of accounting information and under each heading consider the information they might require. Are the accounts likely to give all the information they need?

Summary

This block has shown that the interpretation of accounting information involves analysing **relationships** rather than just considering **absolute figures**. Just as individuals need to consider the wages they earn in relation to what they have to give up in terms of time and effort, so businesses need to relate their profits to the resources given up to earn them.

This concept can be applied in the measurement of a whole range of relationships used to assess the financial performance of any business.

Block 9
Cost Accounting

Cost accounting is the branch of accounting concerned with providing information to 'internal users' of accounting information—basically managers. Cost accounting is really part of management accounting in that it is part of an information system in business that applies knowledge of costs to decisions and gives details of the costs of operating segments or divisions of a business and the costs of producing each product or activity.

'Cost' is a term that seems to have a quite specific meaning, and in some cases this is true. If you buy a piece of furniture for £100 then the cost to you is simply £100. The term cost is being applied to the purchase price.

The manufacturer of the furniture will also have costs. The costs of the material input to make the furniture plus the costs of converting the material into an acceptable saleable product. Conversion costs will include labour costs and the overheads used such as power, heating, lighting, and depreciation of machinery.

In effect the manufacturer is adding value at each stage of the conversion by applying skills and processes.

'Cost' to the manufacturer needs to be carefully defined. Important questions to determine 'cost' would be:

How are the material costs arrived at?
How are labour costs analysed so that the wage costs applicable to each product are known?
How are overhead costs calculated?

This last point about overhead costs introduces the two main costing approaches that need to be appreciated.

Full absorption costing

This is the system of cost accounting that attempts to absorb **all** of a business's costs into the cost of each product produced or each area of activity that a business undertakes.

Costs are either **direct** or **indirect**. Direct costs are the specific costs incurred in producing a product or carrying out a particular activity. Indirect costs are the costs not specifically associated with each activity but costs of operating the business generally.

Rent, rates, heating, insurance, telephone bills, and depreciation are examples of indirect costs.

Activity 1

List the costs that you think would be direct in a business making

a Furniture
b Beer
c Stationery and Greeting Cards

Activity 2

Now list the indirect costs that might be incurred in these businesses.

Indirect costs are also called **overheads**, and in a manufacturing business these costs are as important as the direct costs in enabling firms to produce products. Absorption costing attempts to include in each product's cost an amount for overheads. This is done by setting overhead absorption rates.

Setting absorption rates involves two important activities. First, estimating the overhead costs to be incurred during the coming accounting period. Second, the expected production activity or output needs to be estimated, so that the overhead costs can be spread over this output.

Illustration

A business making valves, junctions and adaptors has these figures:

	Valves	*Junctions*	*Adaptors*
Expected output	2,000	3,000	15,000
Production time to make each one	2 hrs	½ hr	1 hr
Total expected hours to be worked	4,000 hrs	1,500 hrs	15,000 hrs
Total hours of production	20,500		

Expected Overhead Costs	£
Rent	3,200
Rates	2,700
Heating	1,200
Lighting	800
Depreciation	6,600
Staff salaries	24,200
Telephone	1,700
Insurance	600
Total overheads	£41,000

The £41,000 is the expected overhead costs that need to be spread in to the cost of each unit of output so an 'absorption' rate is arrived at of

$$\frac{\text{Estimated overhead £41,000}}{\text{Estimated production hours 20,500}}$$

Therefore £2 per productive hour is the absorption rate, meaning that each time a product is made it will collect or absorb £2 of overhead into its cost, so the cost for overhead of each of the three products is

	Valve		*Junction*		*Adaptor*	
	2 hrs @ £2 =	£4	½ hr @ £2 =	£1	1 hr @ £2 =	£2
The direct costs of each can then be added, for example						
Direct Material		£2		£3		£4
Direct Labour	2 hrs @ £4 =	£8	½ hr @ £4 =	£2	1 hr @ £4 =	£4
Total Cost		£14		£6		£10

These total costs are the fully absorbed costs including overheads. For businesses that have several departments and divisions it is possible to have a separate absorption rate in each department. As products spend time in each department they collect overhead costs. There is some difficulty in setting absorption rates in each department as the exact amount of overhead to be incurred in each can never be accurately ascertained. Many overhead costs are incurred for the business as a whole and are difficult to charge to any one division or department.

The procedures used to spread overhead costs are called **allocation** and **apportionment**. An overhead cost that can be charged specifically to one department is said to be allocated, whereas more general overhead costs, which have to be be arbitrarily charged to various departments, are said to be apportioned. This means that costs like rent, rates, and heating are spread to each department or apportioned by means of an estimate. Usual methods of estimation include the floor area occupied for premises costs like rent, rates, heating, lighting, etc. Costs such as management salaries might be apportioned on the basis of the number of employees in each department or the number of hours worked.

Setting overhead absorption rates would then involve estimating the overhead cost and then spreading it in a fashion similar to that shown in the table that follows.

Item	*Total Cost*	*Machining Dept.*	*Assembly Dept.*	*Painting Dept.*
	£	£	£	£
Rent	3,200	1,600	800	800
Rates	2,700	1,350	675	675
Heating	1,200	600	300	300
Lighting	800	400	200	200
Depreciation	6,600	4,400	1,650	550
Staff Salaries	24,200	11,805	8,263	4,132
Telephone	1,700	850	425	425
Insurances	600	400	150	50
Total	41,000	21,405	21,463	7,132

These apportionments have been made after considering the following information:

1 The machining department uses half of the total space and the other departments use a quarter each.
2 The value of machinery is: £200,000 in the machining department, £75,000 in the assembly department, and £25,000 in the painting department.
3 The expected hours to be worked on production are: 10,000 in the machining department, 7,000 in the assembly department, and 3,500 in the painting department.

The overhead costs need to be spread over the output produced, and one of the more sensible ways is to spread the costs to products on the basis of the time that each product spends in each department in the course of its manufacture. Therefore the absorption rates would be:

	Machining Dept.	*Assembly Dept.*	*Painting Dept.*
Estimated overhead	£21,405	£12,463	£7,132
Estimated production hours	10,000	7,000	3,500
Absorption rates	£2.14	£1.78	£2.04

The business will need to have details of the productive time used by each product in each department. The absorption rates can be applied to the time taken to build up a total overhead charge for each product.

Activity 3

Discuss with other students the problems in spreading overhead costs to the various departments that may exist in different businesses.

Make a list of the costs you would expect to find in businesses from different industries.

The illustration used above is an example of a manufacturing business, but the concept of cost apportionment is equally applicable in all businesses, and equally problematic in each. If the costs of a department have been charged on a basis that has been decided upon by the accountant, it is difficult to see how costs can be controlled by the departmental manager. It is equally difficult to see how arbitrarily charged costs could be a sensible basis for making decisions on the profitability of products or divisions of a business.

Much more knowledge about cost behaviour is needed. Are costs 'fixed' or 'variable'? If they are variable in the sense that they increase with activity, then what measurement of a firm's activity causes the cost increase? Before dwelling on this important aspect we will look finally at cost apportionment for a business totally different from the manufacturing company used in the illustration, namely a sports and leisure centre.

A local authority has borrowed one million pounds at 14% interest to enable it to build a sports complex. The complex consists of several activities listed below:

Cost Centre

1 Badminton Area
2 Squash Courts
3 Swimming Pool
4 Diving Pool
5 Weight Training Area
6 Snack Bar
7 Licensed Bar
8 Administration

The recreation committee of the local authority has prepared the following estimates for the first full year of operation.

Cost Centre	*Budgeted Income*	*Staff Salaries*
	£000s	*£000s*
1	30,000	2,000
2	40,000	3,000
3	25,000	18,000
4	5,000	4,000
5	8,000	7,000
6	12,000	5,000
7	20,000	9,000
8		34,000
Totals	140,000	82,000

Other Operating Costs	£
Rent and rates	8,000
Security	9,400
Chemicals for pools	2,200
Maintenance	6,500
Provisions for Snack Bar	2,000
Provisions for Licenced Bar	6,000
Telephone	2,100
Insurance	1,900

The initial capital cost of one million pounds is deemed to have been spent as follows:

Cost Centre	£000s
1	50
2	230
3	350
4	150
5	20
6	70
7	80
8	50

The floor area occupied by each activity is:

Cost Centre	Square metres
1	1,500
2	2,000
3	1,500
4	500
5	200
6	150
7	150
8	200

Activity 4

Prepare a statement showing the anticipated surplus or deficit for the sports complex, analysing the results by each of the cost centres. Important questions to consider are:

1 How to deal with cost centre 8; the administration department. This is essentially a 'service department' providing a service to the other areas of activity. There is perhaps little choice but to decide on an equitable way to spread the costs of this department to the other departments.

2 Should the interest payment be included in the costs of the sports complex?

3 Your 'judgements' will influence the surplus or deficit of each activity. Is this a fair way to base decisions on the profitability or otherwise of each activity?

Marginal costing

The activity just completed has given no regard to the nature of type of cost under consideration. 'Cost behaviour' is all-important when a variety of business decisions are under review. Full absorption costing attempts to spread **all costs** into the cost of each activity or product without regard to whether the cost is a specific cost of that activity or an arbitrarily spread portion of a total cost.

Costs may be analysed according to their behaviour. In simple terms this means either fixed or variable behaviour.

A **fixed cost** is a cost that remains constant irrespective of the quantity or volume produced or sold.

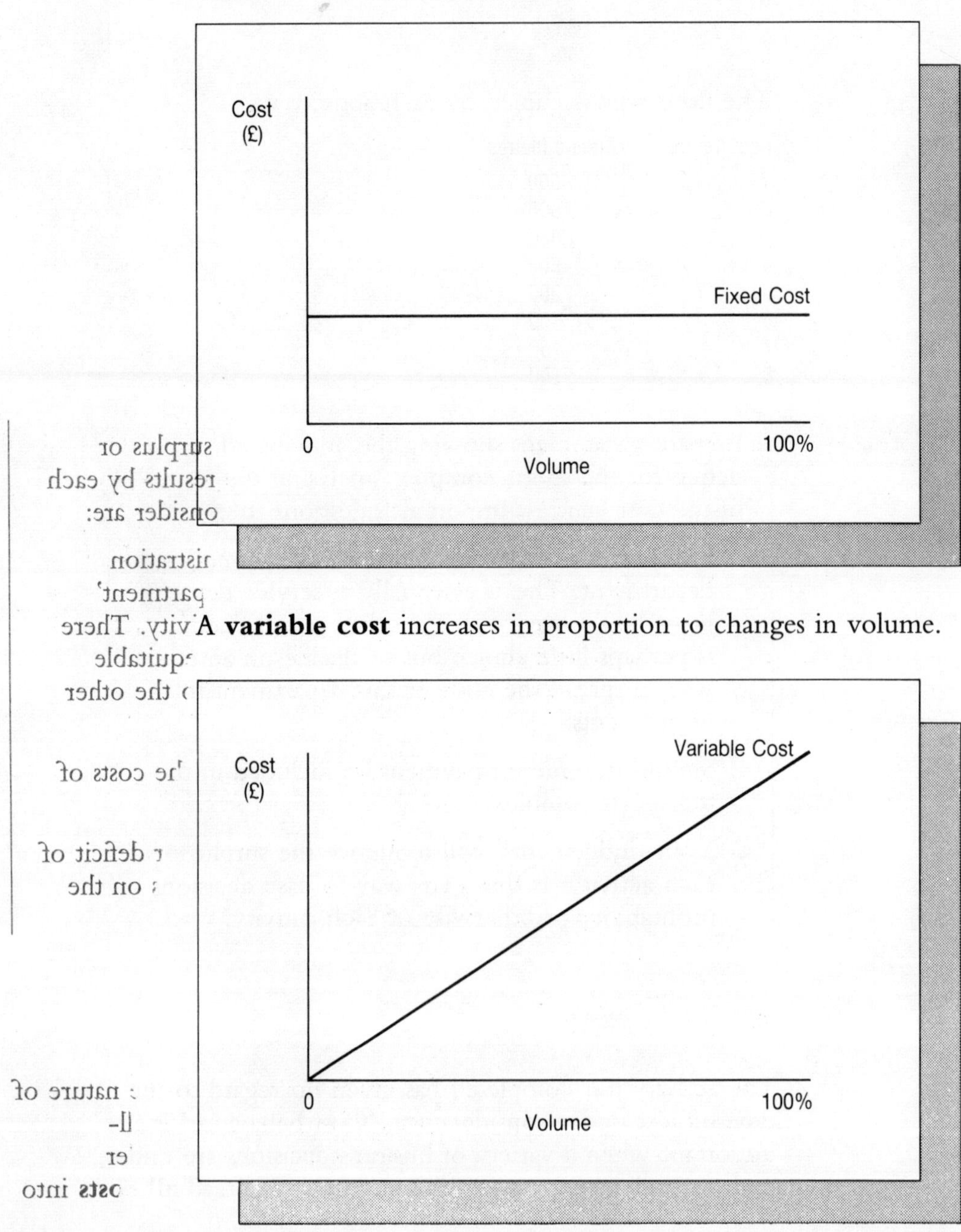

A **variable cost** increases in proportion to changes in volume.

This somewhat simplistic view of cost behaviour ignores the situations where cost does not behave in either of these two ways. Semi-variable costs are those that have an element that remains fixed, but have some degree of variability as well. The following patterns are all displaying semi-variable costs.

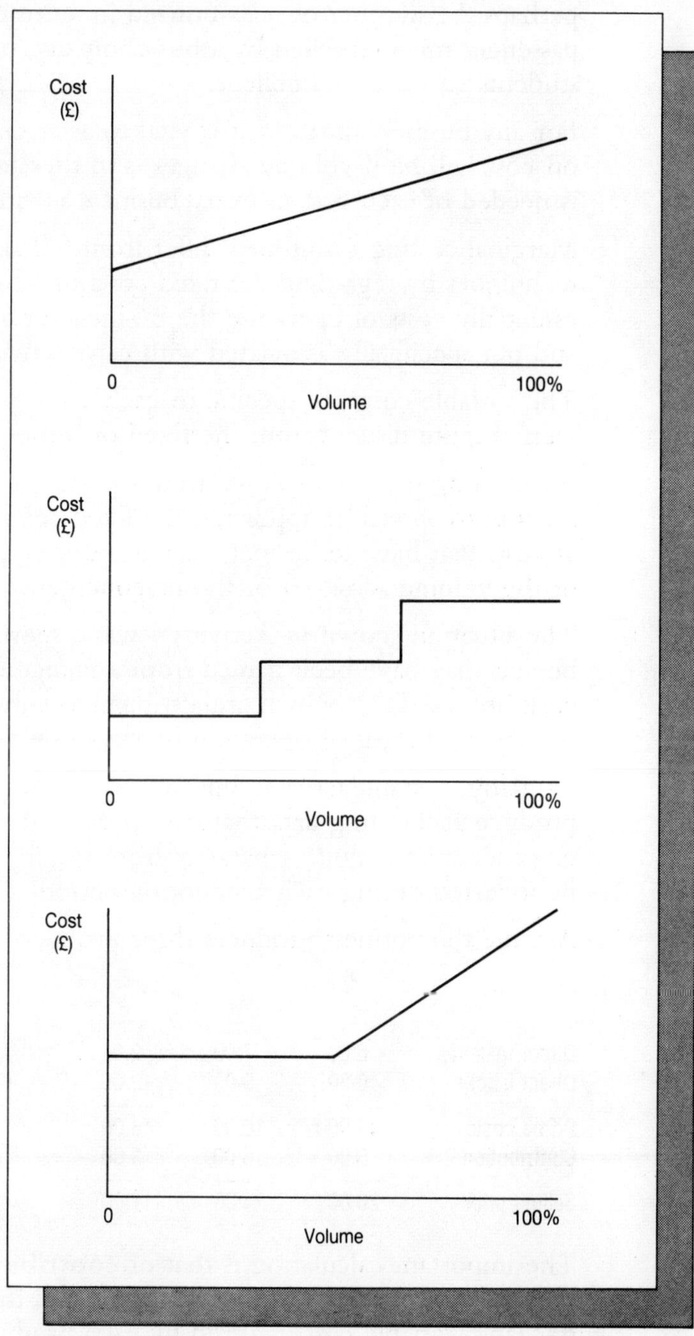

The exact cost that 'fits' each of these charts will depend on the business being considered and the definition of 'volume'. Is volume measured as sales volume? Production units? Productive hours? In fact any other feature that signifies the quantity of activity achieved? Service industries would need to use the feature that is peculiar to their business to measure volume, in perhaps the number of seats utilized in a theatre, the number of passenger miles travelled by a bus company, or the number of students enrolled in a college.

For any business situation it is vital to appreciate what the effect on cost will be if volume changes, and therefore a precise study is needed of each cost in every business situation.

Marginal costing techniques differ from full absorption costing techniques by regarding the fixed costs of a business as essentially costs of operating the business for a period of time and not specifically associated with each activity undertaken.

The variable costs are specific to each activity and should be seen as quite distinct from the fixed or 'time period costs'.

Accounting statements illustrate this point by making no attempt to spread or apportion the fixed costs but to show them as costs that have to be met each accounting period irrespective of the volume achieved or the revenue generated.

The situation shown in Activity 4 was a sports complex, and benefit may have been gained from a recognition of which costs are fixed and which are attributable quite specifically to the different areas of operation in this business situation.

Similarly, a manufacturing business using marginal costing will produce accounting data that has considered the specific activity or product costs quite separately from the fixed costs that will be incurred during each accounting period.

Assume the business produces three products

	X	*Y*	*Z*
	£	£	£
Direct material	8.00	7.00	2.00
Direct labour	6.00	9.00	12.00
Prime costs	14.00	16.00	14.00
Contribution	6.00	8.00	3.00
Selling price	20.00	24.00	17.00

The important calculation is that of **contribution**—the difference between the revenue earned and the specific, traceable variable cost incurred by each product. This contribution goes towards paying off the fixed costs of the business—what is left is profit.

Therefore if the volume produced and sold of each product is

		X	*Y*	*Z*
		3,000	5,000	8,000
Contribution is:		£18,000	£40,000	£24,000
Total contribution	£82,000			
If fixed costs are	£32,000			
then **profit** is	£50,000			

If the fixed costs are £32,000 for this accounting period, the costs of rent, rates, heating, staff salaries, etc. that are included would have to be met irrespective of the volume produced and sold; therefore, any spreading of this fixed overhead over the three products would give results that could mislead if volumes changed. Essentially the £32,000 would remain as a cost even if different quantities were made and sold for any of the products.

Any apportionment of the fixed overhead would be arbitrary and based on estimates and judgements. Objective assessment of the true worth of each activity is needed with costs being recognized as either those that are quite specific to the activity or product or else general for the benefit of the whole business.

In the illustration, each product is generating a contribution and is therefore a worthwhile product in financial terms. Generally any activity is worthwhile if it brings in a contribution. The only time that this may not be the case is if resources used on an activity could have been used elsewhere to generate larger contribution. This would mean that there is an 'opportunity cost' of carrying out production in one area because by so doing more profitable activities are lost elsewhere.

To summarize the basic marginal costing concept we can display the figures used in the example in the form of a simple equation to show the important relationships between revenue, contribution, and profit, thus

sales revenue – variable cost =

$$S - V =$$

contribution = fixed costs + profit

$$C = F + P$$

In the illustration, sales revenue is

Product	X	3,000 units × £20 =	£60,000
	Y	5,000 units × £24 =	£120,000
	Z	8,000 units × £17 =	£136,000
Total			£316,000

Variable costs are

Product	X	3,000 units × £14 =	£42,000
	Y	5,000 units × £16 =	£80,000
	Z	8,000 units × £14 =	£112,000
Total			£234,000

Therefore **sales – variable costs = contribution**

X	£60,000 – £42,000 =	£18,000
Y	£120,000 – £80,000 =	£40,000
Z	£136,000 – £112,000 =	£24,000
Total		£82,000

less fixed costs	£50,000
= Profit	£32,000

Activity 5

List the costs that you would classify as fixed, variable, or semi-variable in the following businesses:

1 Theatre

2 Sports centre

3 Manufacturer of products made from plastic

4 College

5 Coach tour operator

To be more specific about costs that so far have been classified as just 'fixed', it is important to appreciate that there are categories within the generic term of fixed costs. In some businesses that have quite separate divisions, it may be important for the management to see that some fixed costs are specific to each division while others are essentially fixed for the business as a whole. In the block on 'Control' the point will be made that managers have to be held accountable for the costs under their control but not all costs are controllable and for some levels of management certain costs have to be seen as uncontrollable, in the sense that action by the manager could not be expected to significantly alter or reduce the cost.

These sort of fixed costs are called **committed** fixed costs because the business is committed to them by the nature, style, and size of the firm. Other fixed costs may be capable of some degree of control, because decisions as to the amount spent on them are made periodically. Costs like advertising and staff training would come into this category.

The important point is that by highlighting fixed costs in accounting statements as **total** costs that have to be met from contributions from activities before profits are made, management attention is drawn to the cost, and action can be taken on specific controls that may be appropriate for the costs that are included under the general heading of **fixed**.

Activity 6

A business has a profit requirement of £70,000. Its fixed costs are £37,000 with sales planned as follows:

To Company A	20,000 units	@	£5 each
To Company B	10,000 units	@	£5.50 each
To Company C	8,000 units	@	£6.00 each

The variable cost of each unit is £3 and the maximum capacity of the business is 50,000 units. If the firm wishes to operate at full capacity and sell all of the output what is the minimum selling price that should be charged for the uncommitted production in order that the profit requirement is met?

Activity 7

Make a list of the major differences between full absorption costing and marginal costing.

The Profit and Loss Account shown below for the JB Company was produced using full absorption costing. Reproduce it using a marginal costing format. Consider specifically the action that may be necessary regarding product C.

		Products		
	Total	*A*	*B*	*C*
	£	£	£	£
Sales	100,000	60,000	25,000	15,000
Variable costs	60,000	35,000	14,000	11,000
Fixed costs	20,000	8,000	7,000	5,000
Total costs	80,000	43,000	21,000	16,000
Profit	20,000	17,000	4,000	(1,000)

In your marginal costing presentation you will have shown the contribution earned by each product and hopefully you can represent this contribution as a percentage of sales—the contribution to sales ratio or contribution margin.

Activity 8

The following memorandum has been prepared and sent to you for action.

Super Containers PLC

Internal Memorandum

From: P. Maxwell
Chief Accountant

Date: 19th January 19X8
REF: PM/CE

To: P. Boswell
Financial Trainee

Subject: Selling Prices for next year

Further to a budgeting exercise which shows that we should achieve a profit of £50,000 next year, our Sales Manager has suggested that research shows that a 5% reduction in selling price should increase quantity sold by 50%. Because we need very urgently to sell our spare capacity we shall have to examine this possibility very seriously. I am very uncertain that this large increase in quantity is possible, but to assist me in my discussions with the Sales Manager, would you prepare a Profit Forecast based on these estimates, taking into account inflation which is expected to increase material costs by 10% and labour costs by 5%. Overhead costs are also expected to increase by 10%. The budgeted results without any of these changes are as follows:

	£	£
Sales	—	160,000
Direct materials	50,000	
Direct labour	25,000	
Variable overhead	15,000	
Fixed overhead	20,000	110,000
Profit		50,000

Prepare a response to this memorandum considering both the financial and marketing implications.

Break-even Analysis

Given the knowledge of cost behaviour necessary to operate any business, it is important for accountants to be able to express and display data in a meaningful way so that users can be informed in a manner that is helpful to them.

One possible way is by presenting data on charts. This method is particularly useful to show the relationship between a firm's revenue, costs, and profit. Earlier in this block we looked at cost in relation to volume. If sales revenue is also included in the relationship, the profit that results can be depicted on a chart as is shown in the following illustration:

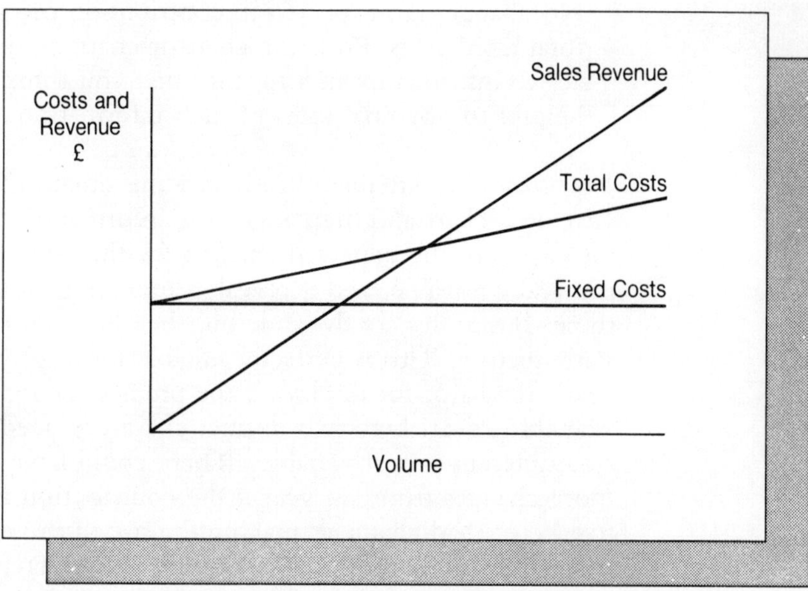

No more information is gained from the presentation than could have been ascertained from a tabulation of revenues and costs at different volume levels, but this form of presentation is an additional weapon in the armory of accountants which helps to display relationships to users in a more interesting manner. In the chart above, as volume increases, so does revenue, and where the revenue line crosses the total cost line is the point at which the firm makes neither profit nor loss and therefore breaks even. As volume and revenue increase so does profit and the pictorial presentation of this can be a useful guide in planning.

Activity 9

A business has three main areas of activity for which the revenues earned last year, the contribution margins, and the profits are given below.

Activity	Contribution margin	Sales revenue
		£
Hire Fleet	50%	60,000
Manufacture	40%	30,000
Sub contract	20%	10,000

Fixed costs for the business as a whole are £24,000. For the coming year, budgets show that sales revenue will increase to £120,00 with the split of sales expected to be.

	£
Hire Fleet	40,000
Manufacture	40,000
Sub contract	40,000

No changes are expected in contribution margins or in total fixed costs. Present a chart or charts to display the above information in a manner that you think would be helpful to potential users of such information.

You may have attempted to depict the situation for the past year on a chart and then adjust the information shown to take into account the expected changes for the coming year. This is not really possible, and it reveals a limitation of charts such as these. Businesses are dynamic but the chart can only represent a static picture. This is perfectly suitable for displaying either last year's results or for displaying the predictions for the coming year. However, here two distinct charts are needed to display two different sets of variables. There could have been even more changes from last year if the contribution margins or the fixed costs had changed, making the use of the charts even more difficult as many different lines would have been necessary. Being aware of limitations is not the same as saying that charts are unsuitable for displaying relationships that may be subject to changes. However, the use of charts requires careful analysis of business costs and revenues, and a recognition that such relationships are rarely static.

An alternative presentation of the chart would be as follows:

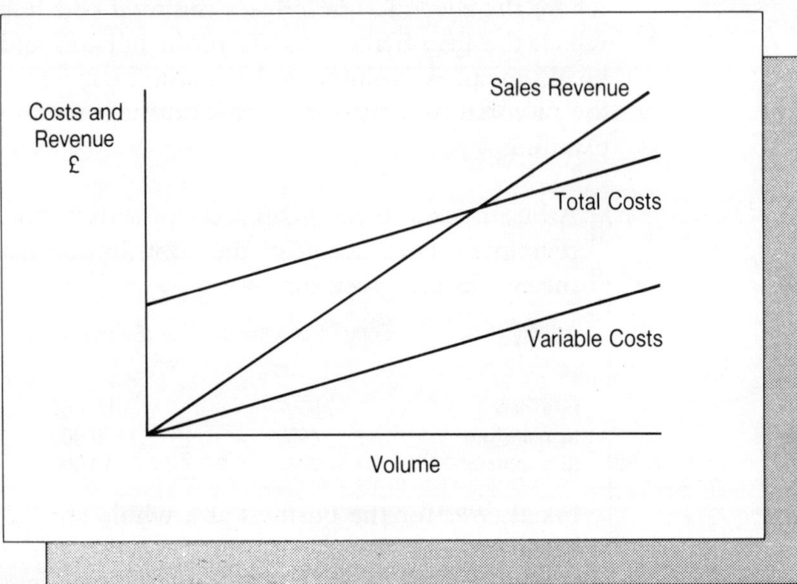

Activity 10

What differences are there in this chart to the one shown on page 149?
What additional information is revealed?

What you should have seen is that **contribution** is revealed by this presentation. By plotting revenue as the function that increases with volume and then variable costs that also increase with volume, the gap that appears is the contribution that is earned at different volume levels thus:

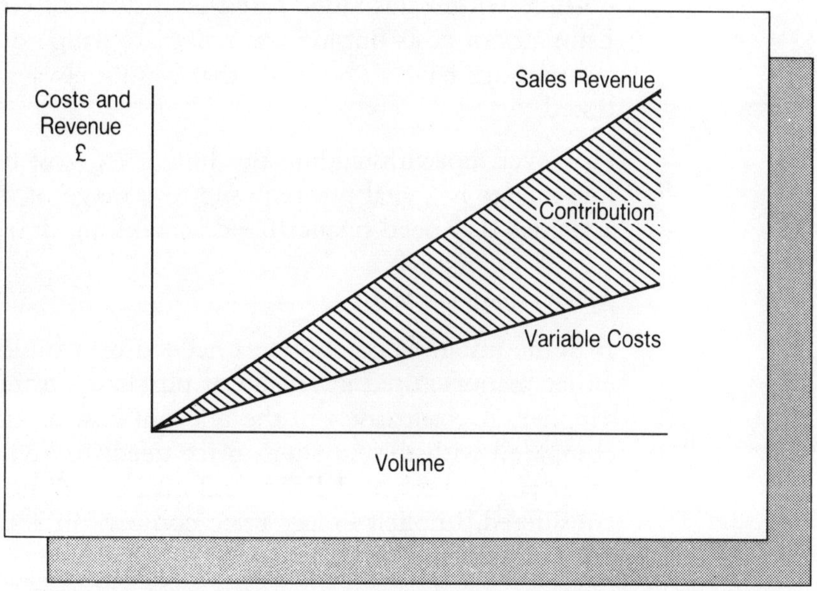

The chart shown on page 150 has the fixed costs added to the variable costs to give a total costs line, thus revealing profit.

In your studies of The Organization in its Environment, and the Economics Sections in this unit, you have no doubt considered costs and revenue relationships in a business. It is unlikely that economists' charts would show as many straight lines as the charts shown in this block. Economists usually put forward theories of supply and demand and pricing structure, but these theories need to be tested in specific businesses.

The concept of diminishing returns may well be generally appreciated but whether the general concept is applicable in a specific firm is the concern of that firm's management and it will need to be tested and measured over the more narrow range of the firm's activities. The term 'Relevant Range' is often used to illustrate cost behaviour in a specific business. This term means that generalized views that permeate discussions on costs need to be carefully considered in a specific context. For instance a cost may be totally fixed, and unaffected by changes in volume or output within the range of activities normally undertaken by a firm. Outside this known range, costs are not known, and care is needed when assessing whether changes are likely.

Essentially then, if a firm operates within a known range of normal activity, say, for instance, 60% volume at the lowest level and 85% at the normal highest level, cost predictions are possible within this range based on a study of cost records. Estimates of costs outside this range are dangerous, as assumptions have to be made that cannot always be easily tested.

However, notwithstanding this limitation, cost behaviour knowledge is a vital pre-requisite to a range of decision-making activities that need financial and accounting data as a basis.

Make or buy decisions

In some instances components needed by a business can be either manufactured internally or purchased from an outside supplier. A comparison of the relevant cost of manufacturing compared with the supplier's price needs to be made, and then other factors such as delivery and quality will need to be considered. Implicit in any price comparison is that 'the relevant cost can be ascertained'.

Activity 11

What do you consider the term 'relevant cost' to mean? Which costs should be included and which excluded?

Closure or abandonment decisions

Should a firm close down a particular division or activity? What are the costs involved and what costs are likely to be saved?

Activity 12

Discuss with other students the criteria that should be used for decisions such as this. Include social criteria as well as cost information.

Product or activity mix decisions

How should resources of labour and machinery be deployed in a business? Which activities should receive resources in the form of time and facilities, and how should a sensible mix of products or activities be achieved?

Activity 13

List the criteria that you think should form the basis of decisions like these. How would you go about collecting the required information?

What these activities show is that there is a wide variety of decisions that have to be made in business, requiring a knowledge of the effect on costs. There will be many other factors to consider, often requiring judgement by management. Financial input to a decision is vital but the data itself is of little use unless it can be understood and interpreted and augmented by input of a non-financial nature such as sales demand, effects on employment, and technology required.

Finally to return to the break-even charts consider this situation:

Activity 14

The following chart is presented to you when you attend an interview with a manufacturing company. You are asked to consider the following points:

1 The chart has been prepared using the financial results from last year. You are told that for next year, sales volume is budgeted at £95,000 and therefore the 'profit' should be excellent given that last year sales revenue was only £80,000. Prepare a reasoned response to this rather subjective statement.
2 Present the chart with costs displayed in an alternative form.
3 Discuss the advantages that either presentation may have, paying particular attention to the sorts of detail shown on each.
4 Comment on the 'margin of safety' shown on the chart.
5 Suggest any action that could be taken to enable the firm to lower the break-even point.

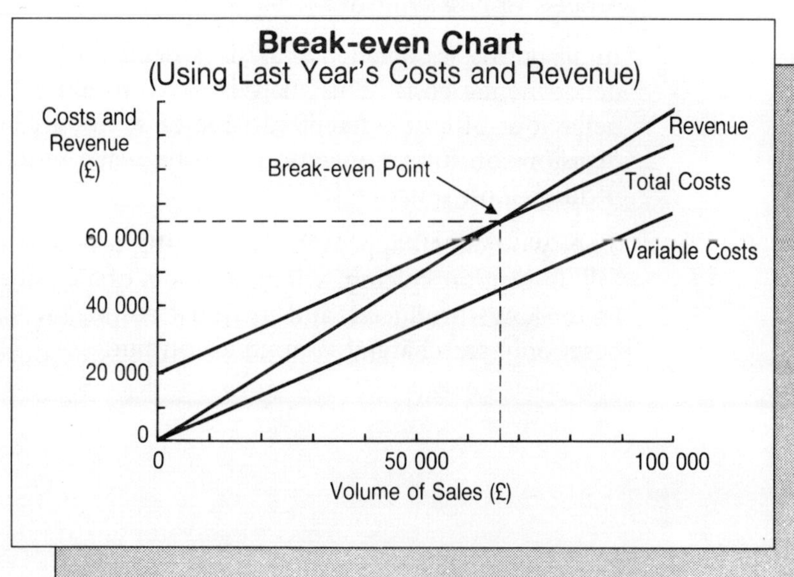

Break-even charts can be used to show the 'what if' decisions. *What if* the sales revenue in the business can be increased by increasing the prices? *What if* variable costs can be decreased by carrying out economies in the manufacturing operations? *What if* fixed costs can be controlled by a programme to reduce heating costs, lighting costs, insurances, etc.?

In fact, any predictions of future business possibilities can be shown on the chart. As was mentioned earlier, the chart is an alternative vehicle for presenting information that may be better understood than a more sterile presentation of figures. Possible future changes can perhaps be visualized more easily with a chart than with tabulated results.

Activity 15

Using the chart from Activity 14, show the effects of the following changes that may occur in the future:

a a 5% decrease in selling prices
b a 2% increase in unit variable costs
c a £1,000 increase in fixed costs
d a £1,000 increase in fixed costs at 75% of total volume produced and sold.

Summary

Cost and management accounting is the part of accounting concerned with measuring the cost of operating areas of business and providing cost data to management as part of the process of cost control.

In all businesses detailed analysis is needed of product and departmental costs. This analysis needs to embrace the behaviour of cost – fixed, variable or semi-variable – so that decisions on future operations can be made with a knowledge of likely cost outcomes.

The two general approaches to costing products or services are full absorption costing, where all costs of a business are spread to the units produced, and marginal costing, where variable costs only are charged to units of output.

Block 10
Control

Accounting is concerned with recording events and transactions and from these records producing statements such as Profit and Loss Accounts and Balance Sheets.

Essentially these statements are recording history—events that have taken place in the past. No doubt owners and managers can learn from history and from accounting statements that are derived from historical data, but once incurred, costs cannot be controlled. Only future events may possibly be controlled.

The question must be: how controlled and by whom? This block looks at the concept of control in the following areas:

1 Control through planning and budgeting, setting budgets for different business areas and preparing accounting statements that compare actual events and costs with the budget.
2 Control of working capital by specific controls over debtors, stock and cash.
3 Control through ratios and performance indicators. The majority of these controls have been outlined in Block 8 on Performance Analysis, but some of the ratios are applicable in the two areas above. Budgetary control techniques are applicable in all businesses, but the degree of detail and the people involved must vary according to the size, nature, and complexity of the business. A small business will need to prepare forecasts or budgets for its major activities—**sales, purchases, operating costs, and cash flow**. Larger businesses will need to budget for these items also, but the degree of detail will be much greater and the purpose will be somewhat different. Most large organizations have complex structures of management. Different managers having different responsibilities for **sales, production, purchasing**, and so on. A budget is a management tool for co-ordinating these different functions. Managers will be accountable or responsible for achieving targets specified in the budget. Their involvement in setting the budget and the action they take to control events, costs, and income to achieve the budgeted target can be seen as part of a management strategy that should operate to achieve success for the business.

In recent years, significant research has been carried out to investigate the success, or otherwise, of budgeting techniques as vehicles for motivating managers. A lot of the research has attempted to measure the success of budgets in helping managers achieve goals. These are often business goals, but may also include their personal goals.

This idea of motivation plays an important part in budgeting and controlling, and can only be ignored at the expense of success.

Budgeting should be seen not just as figure collecting and estimating the future, but as a coherent attempt to organize managers in a systematic way so that sensible and realistic targets can be set that both recognize realities and attempt to stimulate effective performance.

Stages in budgetary control can be seen as

1 **Planning**—preparing targets for each area of business activity.

2 **Co-ordinating**—making sure that each part of a plan fits with other parts, e.g. the sales target and the production budget need to be compatible. It is pointless to budget to sell items that the production department cannot produce.

3 **Recording**—the accounting department, in addition to being involved in recording managers' plans, needs to record actual events in a form that allows comparison.

4 **Controlling**—comparisons of actual with budgeted performance will produce variances or differences. Managers must account for such differences and ensure corrective action takes place.

The planning stage requires a careful look at business activities. What can be sold? What costs will be incurred?

The chart given opposite, shows the sort of budgets that need to be prepared and the links between each budget.

Essentially each budget inter-relates with every other budget and they all form part of the total Master Budget, showing the budgeted Profit and Loss Account and Balance Sheet. The Cash Budget is the prediction of the cash or liquid resources that are expected to be available during the budget period.

Inter-relationship between Budgets

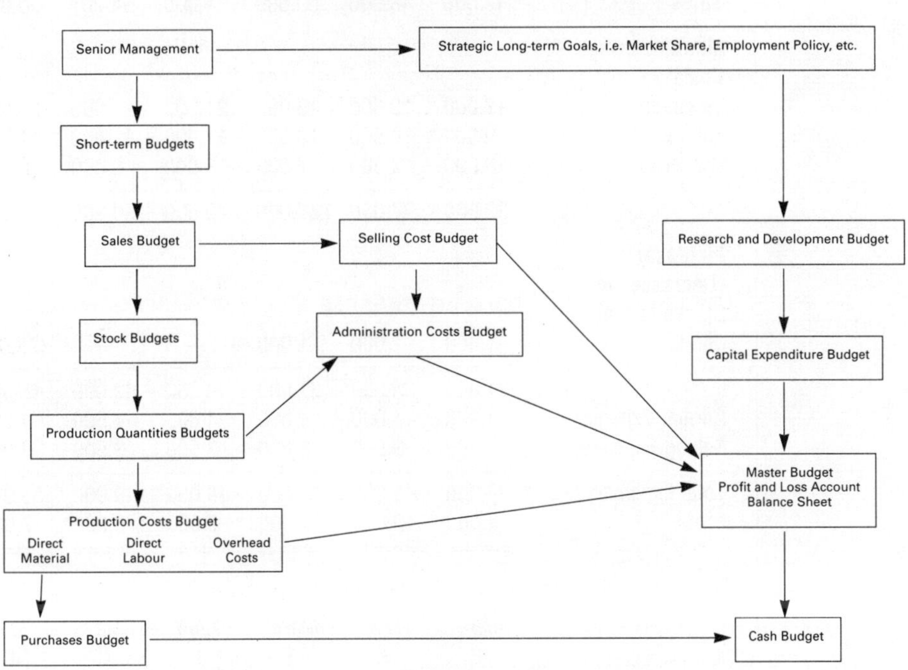

Senior Management

Strategic Long-term Goals, i.e. Market Share, Employment Policy, etc.

Short-term Budgets

Sales Budget

Selling Cost Budget

Research and Development Budget

Stock Budgets

Administration Costs Budget

Capital Expenditure Budget

Production Quantities Budgets

Master Budget
Profit and Loss Account
Balance Sheet

Production Costs Budget
Direct Material Direct Labour Overhead Costs

Purchases Budget

Cash Budget

Cash budgeting is a critical activity in every business. Businesses must have liquid resources available to finance their activities. Cash is part of working capital and needs to be planned. There is a difference between profit and cash, and each needs management attention to ensure that strategies are employed to achieve these two distinct controllable features.

The Finance book has a block called Cash Control (Block 3) and a section on Cash Budgets (page 18). The cash budget shown is for the personal finances of a family, detailing sources of income—salary, etc., and cash outgoings to pay for mortgage, electricity, and general living expenses. The logic contained in this activity is equally applicable to businesses.

Activity 1

The budgets on page 158 have been prepared for a manufacturing business and your task is to prepare a month-by-month cash budget showing the inflows and outflows of cash.

The Cash Balance on January 1st is expected to be £3,000.

	Jan. £	*Feb.* £	*March* £	*April* £	*May* £	*June* £
Sales	42,000	48,000	50,000	54,000	54,000	60,000
Manufacturing Costs						
Materials	17,000	19,000	20,000	21,000	21,000	23,000
Labour	9,000	10,500	10,500	11,000	11,000	11,500
Overhead	6,000	7,500	7,500	8,000	8,000	8,500
	32,000	37,000	38,000	40,000	40,000	43,000
Increase/ (Decrease) in Stocks of finished goods	1,000	1,000	1,000	—	—	(2,000)
	31,000	36,000	37,000	40,000	40,000	45,000
Admin. Expenses	4,000	4,000	4,000	4,500	4,500	4,000
Selling Expenses	3,000	3,000	3,000	3,500	3,500	3,500
Total Expenses	38,000	43,000	44,000	48,000	48,000	53,000
Profit	4,000	5,000	6,000	6,000	6,000	7,000

The material cost charge is made up of:

	Jan. £	*Feb.* £	*March* £	*April* £	*May* £	*June* £
Opening Stock	2,000	3,000	4,000	4,000	5,000	4,000
Purchases	18,000	20,000	20,000	22,000	20,000	23,000
	20,000	23,000	24,000	26,000	25,000	27,000
Closing Stock	3,000	4,000	4,000	5,000	4,000	4,000
	17,000	19,000	20,000	21,000	21,000	23,000

Materials purchased are paid for in the month following delivery. In December purchases were £16,000.

On average, 50% of the debtors pay the month after being invoiced, 50% in the subsequent month.

Sales for the previous November and December were £44,000 and £40,000 respectively.

The manufacturing overheads include depreciation at £1,000 per month, and it can be assumed that payments for overheads are made in the month in which they occur.

Corporation Tax is payable in January of £510,000.

In February £5,000 will be paid for a new machine. In March £2,500 will be paid for a new delivery van.

What action would you expect the company to take in light of the cash budget?

The main features to note are that, although the detailed budgets for sales and costs show that profits are expected for each of the first six months of the coming year, the cash situation is not so healthy. Budgeted Profit and Loss Accounts reflect accounting concepts in the treatment of depreciation, whereas when planning cash, the full capital expenditure needs to be considered. Depreciation is not a cash cost. Corporation tax on previous years' profits has to be found from cash resources during this period under consideration and this will not appear as a cost in the Profit and Loss Accounts—it is an appropriation from the profits earned. The two items of capital expenditure will not appear on the budgeted Profit and Loss Accounts; only the depreciation charges will appear as costs, in line with accounting convention.

Activity 2

From the following data prepare a month-by-month cash budget for the months of January, February, and March.

Expected cash balance January 1st: £32,000.
A new computer installation is planned for January at a cost of £110,000, this is to be paid for in March.
Tax of £170,000 is to be paid in February.
Sales commission of 2% on sales is to be paid one month after the month of sale.
Under an agreement whereby company cars are leased, a payment of £10,000 a month has to be made.
On average, suppliers allow two months credit.
In February £50,000 is expected from debentures.
In January the dividend to ordinary shareholders of £45,000 is to be paid.
Production overheads include depreciation of £2,000 a month.
Wages and overhead costs are paid during the month in which they appear in the Profit and Loss Account.
Sales revenue is received after giving customers one month credit on average. Sales for December were £190,000.

	October £	*November* £	*December* £	*January* £	*February* £	*March* £
Direct Materials	50,000	45,000	60,000	40,000	30,000	36,000
Direct Wages	40,000	36,000	44,000	32,000	25,000	28,000
Overheads:						
Production	16,000	13,000	17,000	19,000	15,000	17,000
Admin.	8,000	9,000	11,000	11,000	10,000	11,000
Selling	5,000	6,000	6,000	5,000	6,000	5,000
Distribution	4,000	5,000	6,000	6,000	5,000	5,000
Sales	150,000	195,000	230,000	200,000	190,000	170,000

Activity 3

The Cash Budget prepared in Activity 2 shows the expected cash balances at the end of each month. Profit planning may reveal very different figures for each month. List the reasons why profit and cash can be so different.

In Block 12 of *Finance* which gives interviews with people involved with finance and accounting there is a detailed account of a credit controller (p. 185). It may help if you read through this interview as it explains how time and effort have to be spent in chasing payments from customers. It is a basic feature of accounting statements that sales revenue will have been charged in the Profit and Loss Accounts when the sale is made even though cash may not be received for some considerable time.

This leads to a discussion of working capital generally, with cash and debtors being part of the working capital of any business. Balance sheets will be concerned with listing current assets and current liabilities and therefore detailing the working capital figure as at balance sheet date. Recording working capital is very different from controlling working capital, and in looking at the second area of control it is important to consider the specific working capital controls that can be engineered. Current assets will be

stocks
debtors
cash at bank.

Current liabilities are those liabilities that have to be met quickly, such as most trade creditors. The difference between current assets and current liabilities is working capital. Knowing this figure at the year end balance sheet date may be all that is necessary to satisfy the reporting requirements of a business, but for control purposes, more regular information will be needed. The chart opposite shows how working capital circulates in a business.

Activity 4

The chart opposite relates to a manufacturing business. Prepare a flow of working capital similar to this for a retail business. Discuss with other students why there may be a difference in flow between the two types of business.

Too much money tied up in working capital can be very wasteful as there are usually better ways to invest capital than to tie it up in stocks which may have long shelf lives, or in debtors, that may take some time to be converted into more liquid funds. Obviously firms needs to hold stocks, and money

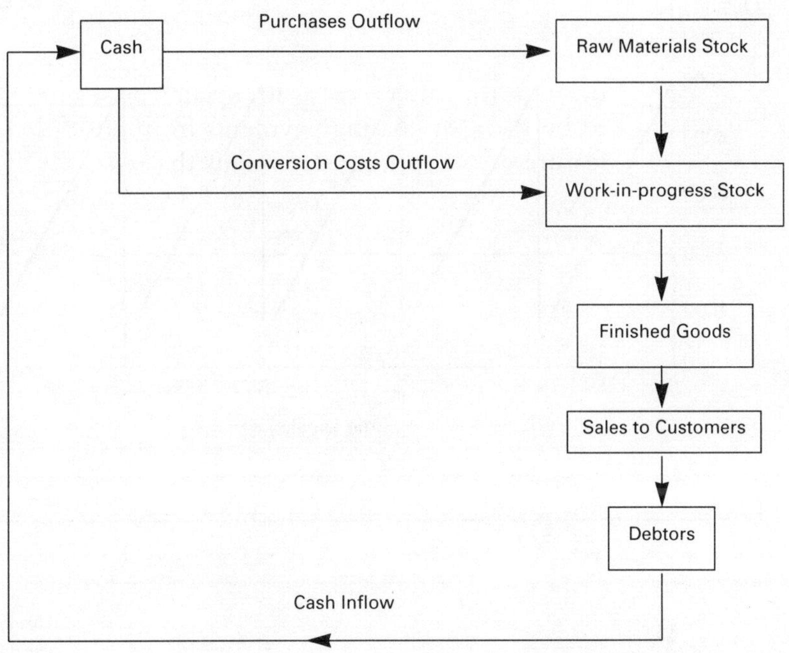

outstanding in customers' hands is perhaps an inevitable part of trading. However, your capital in someone else's bank gives your business no benefit at all. Similarly, too much capital tied up in stock is wasteful. There will be an opportunity cost of lost interest plus the attendant cost of storage and administration. Controls are needed in the following areas:

1 Stock control
2 Debtor control
3 Cash control—the details of this have been given in the first part of this block.

Stock control means ensuring that there is adequate availability of stock in the right place at the right time and with the minimum amount of capital tied up. Most businesses need to keep a wide variety of stock, and investment at an adequate level is vital. However, what is adequate can only be determined with a knowledge of demand, availability of supply, and information about price movements.

The following charts represent movement and replacement of stock.

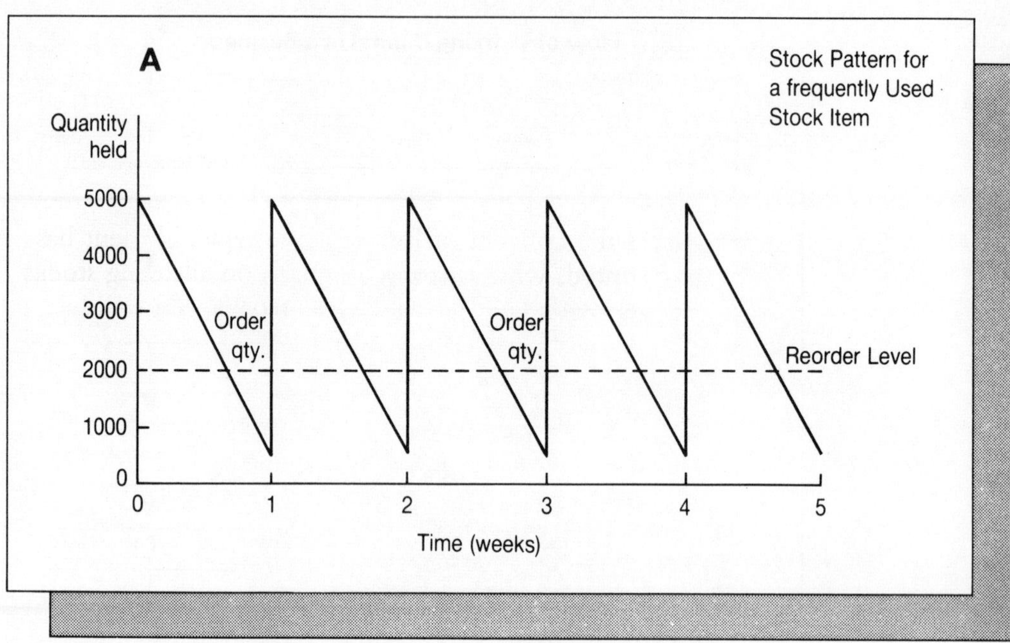

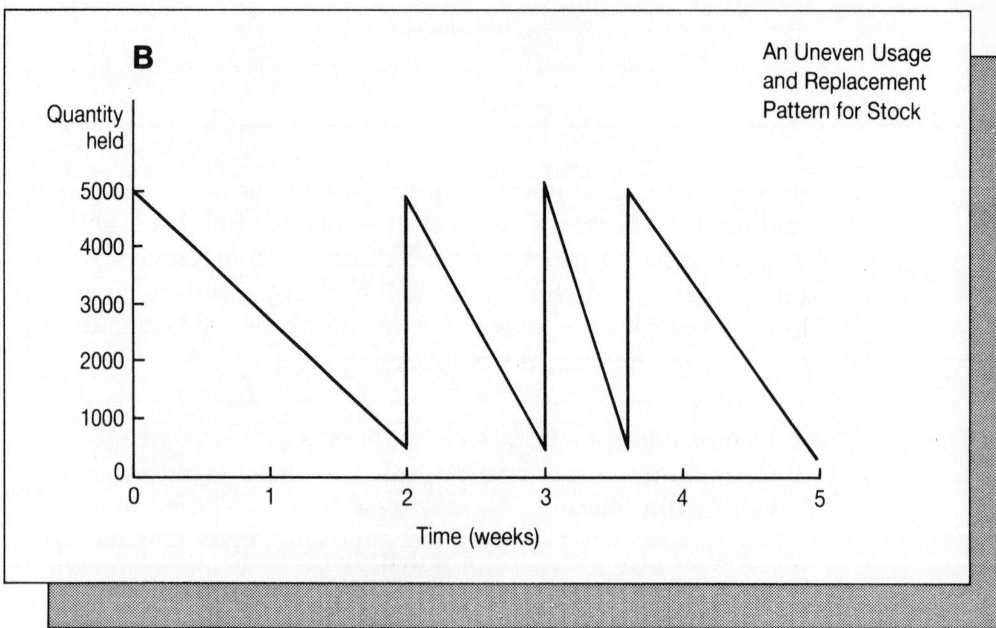

These two different usage and replacement patterns show how difficult it is to generalize about stock control. The first item of stock shows a steady rate of consumption, and even re-ordering patterns. The second shows irregular usage that complicates decisions about replacement, both in terms of when to order and the amounts to re-order.

It always aids stock control if supplies are known, and usage and delivery is fairly constant. However, businesses have to operate with the problem of holding a vast array of different stocks all with different rates of usage and replenishment, making decisions on stock control difficult.

In recent times the concept of Just in Time replenishment has been much vaunted, with a strong emphasis on allowing stocks to fall to a level that some may perceive as dangerously low, but, by doing so, enabling working capital to be retained in the business for as long as possible.

Activity 5

List the factors that you think would determine an economic order quantity when replacing stock.

Activity 6

Accountants often calculate ratios to measure efficiency and performance (see Block 8) and stock utilization is a prime area for measuring efficiency. List and discuss the types of control that you think would be important for businesses to exercise over materials. Pay particular emphasis to ratios that could be calculated and the controls that should be used for purchasing, storage, and usage.

Debtor Control

Control over money outstanding from customers is vital, and ratios may help in attempting to assess the effectiveness of controls. Some firms calculate debts outstanding in terms of 'number of sales days outstanding'.

This helps to highlight the fact that cash in the hands of customers represents sales that have been made and are not yet benefiting the business. Real control is not exercised by simply listing and analysing debts; good control involves making sure that sales are made to credit-worthy customers and is not about simply chasing overdue accounts.

Activity 7

Discuss with other students the sorts of checks that a business should instigate when dealing with a new customer to ensure credit-worthiness.

Case Study on Working Capital

Tulip PLC is a company that produces a variety of products for the DIY business.

At 31st December 19X7 its balance sheet showed the following:

	£000	£000
Stocks	150	
Debtors	250	400
less Trade creditors		90
Working capital		310
Fixed assets		120
Capital employed		430
Long term loans at 13%		110
Share capital and reserves		160
Bank overdraft		160
		430

The figure given for bank overdraft is a representative figure of the state of the overdraft over the whole of the accounting period. Interest payable is on average 15%.

The Profit and Loss Account for the year ended 31.12.19X7 shows the following:

	£000
Sales revenue	1,100
less Cost of goods sold	710
	390
less Operating costs (rent, rates, heating, etc.)	320
	70
Interest payable	38
Profit before taxation	32

The management team wish to improve profits, and a group is set up to look at selling prices and the possibility of improving revenue by examining prices charged.

A further group is to look at cost control with a view to implementing cost reduction programmes in various areas of the business.

The third group—to which you are seconded—is to look at working capital control with a view to significantly increasing profits by implementing stringent control in this area. A senior member of the group suggests that, given a knowledge of competing businesses, the firm ought to be able to reduce working capital from the present 28% of turnover to a figure 'significantly better than this'.

Your group will look at activities that will improve performance in the following areas:

1 stocks
2 debtors
3 creditors

1 *Stocks*

It is suggested that if stocks are replenished by having a less prudent approach to minimum or safety stocks, there could be a reduction in average stock holding of £20,000. Similarly, a reduction in the safety margin of finished goods stocks could bring about a saving of £20,000 in the amount of stock held. In addition, an attempt to control the build-up of stocks before major orders are undertaken would bring about a saving of £10,000 of stocks held.

In a full year it is expected that these measures will reduce stocks on average by £20,000.

2 *Debtors*

It is anticipated that the following controls will reduce average debtors by £40,000 per annum:

1 Invoicing daily rather than only at month ends.
2 Following up late payments more quickly.
3 Linking sales commissions to payments from customers rather than to deliveries.
4 Initiating cheque collection by some sales representatives rather than relying only on postal payments.

3 *Creditors*

This is one of the most difficult areas, as not paying bills when they become due is exactly the opposite of the credit control policy that the firm wishes to pursue to improve its own debtor control. However, it is decided that with some overseas suppliers, 90 day bills can be used for payment. In addition, some payment terms for home suppliers can be extended. This policy should in a average year increase the level of creditors by £10,000.

Possible results (Only look at this section after working through the case)

Stock reduction	£20,000
Debtor reduction	£40,000
Creditors increase	£10,000
Bank overdraft decrease	£70,000
Interest saved (at 15%)	£10,500
Less implementation costs	£500
Profit improvement	£10,000

The profit of the business has been increased by nearly one-third. This will give a better return on capital employed, and this is in addition to the expected improvements in profits planned for by the other groups.

Summary

Control is an essential feature of any management strategy in business. Financial control involves preparing budgets or targets, comparing control performance with the plans and reporting on differences or variances.

Control is needed over operating costs, performance strategy and working capital. It is not the accountant who is responsible for control but everyone in management who makes any accounting input or interpretation.

Glossary

Accountant

A person involved in the practice of accountancy. The term should only be applied to a person who has successfully completed the examinations and practical experience requirements of one of the four professional accountancy institutes. These are the Institute of Chartered Accountants (ICA), the Chartered Association of Certified Accountants (ACA), the Chartered Institute of Management Accountants (CIMA), and the Chartered Institute of Public Finance and Accountancy (CIPFA). Others working in the areas of finance and accountancy may be qualified as members of the Association of Accounting Technicians (AAT). Accountants tend to specialize in either financial accounting or cost and management accounting.

Accounting, accountancy

The recording, analysis, and presentation of financial data relating to the transactions of an organization in a form which conforms to the practices and conventions of the accountancy profession. All activities relating to the financial aspects of an organization, with regard to historical data, control of current financial matters, and financial planning for the future.

Accounting concepts and conventions

The name given to a series of accepted principles and practices relating to the recording and analysis of financial data, which should be followed in the preparation of all financial statements.

Accruals, or matching, principle

Costs and revenues should be accounted for in the period in which they occur, regardless of when cash changes hands. Any payment in advance for an expense should be excluded from the expenses charged against a particular accounting period, and any amount owing for an expense should be included in the charges made for the period. In this way the profits for a period cannot be manipulated by adjusting the date of payment.

Business entity

Any business is deemed to have an identity which is distinct and separate from that of its owner(s). Financial matters relating to the owner's personal affairs must be kept separate from the business finances at all times.

Consistency convention

Once an accountancy policy has been established by an organization it should be used consistently unless there is good reason for a change. For example, the method of depreciation chosen by a firm should not be changed frequently but should be used consistently.

Cost concept

Assets acquired by an organization should initially be valued at cost, regardless of the apparent market value of the item. If an organization believes it has bought an asset at a bargain price, it should still appear in the books at cost and not at the value which the organization places on it.

Duality concept

Each time a financial transaction occurs, it is recorded in two accounts in the ledger. For every **debit** entry made in a ledger account there is an opposite **credit** entry.

Going concern principle

Books of account should always be prepared on the assumption that the organization is going to continue trading. The affairs of the organization should not appear differently if changes in size, ownership, structure, type of business, or style of trading, are planned for the near future.

Materiality principle

Items which are to be used over a period of time, but which cost only a small amount, will be charged to the period in which they are bought and will not be treated as fixed assets. It would not be appropriate, for example, to treat pencils, rubbers and rulers as fixed assets and therefore to depreciate them over a number of accounting periods. The purchase of this kind of item will simply be charged as an expense in the stationery account.

Money measurement concept

Only items which can be measured in money terms will be shown in the accounts. One of the greatest assets of an organization might be the skills, knowledge and experience of its staff, but since this cannot be valued precisely in money terms it does not appear in the books.

Prudence convention

When a choice has to be made regarding asset values, liability values or estimated expenses, the accountant will always choose that value which shows the organization in the least favourable light. This convention of caution, conservatism and prudence ensures that the true and fair views which the accounts should present do not overstate the well-being of the firm and thus mislead investors or others dealing with it. For example, stock should always be valued at cost or net realizable value, whichever is the lower, thus ensuring that it does not appear at an unrealistically high value in the balance sheet.

Realization concept

Profit is deemed to occur when a sale takes place and not when cash changes hands. Thus if a transaction is on credit the sale is accounted for as having occurred when the goods change hands, and a debt is then formed between buyer and seller which, when settled at a later date, does not produce any profit.

Accruals

An accrual is an amount owed by a business for an expense which has been **consumed** in a financial year and for which payment has not been made. For example, in a financial year which ends on 31st December 19X1, a business may owe £200 in rates to the local authority. This £200 is rates accrued and appears in the balance sheet of the business as a Current Liability.

Acid test ratio

See **Liquid assets ratio**

Assets

An asset is an item with a reasonable financial value which is owned by an organization.

Current assets

Current assets are items which are owned by the organization but which are constantly changing in nature and/or amount. Most organizations classify their current assets as stock, debtors, prepayments, balance at bank, and cash in hand.

Fixed assets

Fixed assets are those items which an organization expects to keep for a long time to assist in its activities, such as buildings, vehicles and machinery. An item is treated as a fixed asset if the organization would not normally trade in such items frequently.

Auditing

Auditing is the process of checking and verifying accounting documents and statements to ensure that they give a 'true and fair' view of the financial affairs of the organization by independent accountants whose competence and integrity give the required credibility to the financial information report.

Average rate of return

A method of assessing the profitability of a proposed project or operation. The average profit per annum is expressed as a percentage of the average capital employed during the life of the project. This enables the manager to rank competing projects in order of predicted profitability. The percentage average rate of return (sometimes known as the **book rate of return**) is calculated as (CE = Capital Employed):

$$\textbf{Average rate of return} = \frac{\textbf{Average annual profit}}{\textbf{(Opening CE + Closing CE)} \div 2} \times 100\%$$

The main weakness of this method of assessing projects is that it ignores the time value of money (which is taken into account when using discounting methods).

Balance sheet

The document which shows the current financial state of an organization. It includes all assets and liabilities of an organization at a given point in time. The account is balanced because capital, the third category of item shown on the balance sheet, is defined as *assets less liabilities*. Thus by displaying assets on one side, opposite capital and liabilities, the accounting equation (capital = assets *less* liabilities) makes the two sides of the balance sheet equal.

The balance sheet is an important document when interpreting the financial affairs of an organization, especially with respect to liquidity, capital structure and gearing.

Bank reconciliation statement

A calculation which reconciles the bank balance shown in an organization's books with that shown on the bank statement. The two figures will rarely coincide because of delays in the presentation of cheques, the transmission of data between bank and client, and various other reasons.

Regular reconciliation of the figures is an important aspect of cash control in any organization.

Bank statement

A document produced by a bank showing all transactions relating to a client's account. It is an extract from the client's account in the bank's book-keeping system.

Book rate of return

See **Average rate of return**

Break-even analysis, break-even chart

The name given to a set of techniques which analyses the behaviour of costs in relation to the level of activity in an organization and establishes the levels required to break even, i.e. to make no loss and no profit. The chart is a useful planning device when using marginal costing techniques to predict the effects of various possible levels of price, cost and volumes of output in future accounting periods.

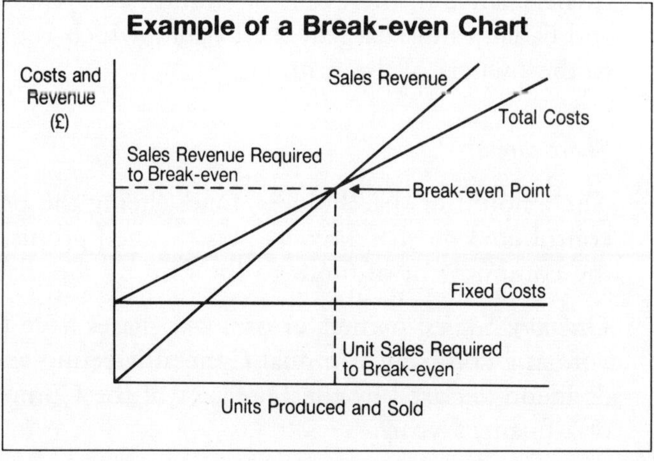

Budgets, budgeting

A budget is a financial statement or plan which is prepared and approved in advance of an accounting period. It may not be a forecast of what is expected to happen but rather a target or objective at which the organization should aim. During the accounting period to which the budget applies, comparison is made between the budget and the actual results attained in order to monitor financial performance.

The CIMA defines budgetary control as, 'The establishment of budgets relating the responsibility of executives to the requirements of a policy, and the continuous comparison of actual with budgeted results, either to secure by individual action the objective of that policy or to provide a basis for its revision'. Thus the monitoring of actual performance and its comparison with the budget is designed to allocate responsibility and increase the accountability of individuals within an organization.

One particularly important section of the budget is the cash budget. This plans an organization's inflows and outflows of cash in order to establish any needs for overdrafts or other forms of borrowing during the coming accounting period.

Capital

Capital = Total assets *less* total liabilities.

When a firm starts up, its capital is the amount of funds invested in its activities by its owner or owners. As profits are earned and retained in the firm ('ploughed back') the capital grows in accordance with the above accounting equation. It may be said to be the amount which the firm owes to its owners, since in the event of closure, after assets are realized and liabilities discharged, the balance which is the capital reverts to the owners of the firm.

Share capital

The amount of shareholders' funds, being the original amount contributed by shareholders plus retained profits, representing the commitment of funds to the firm by the shareholders.

Ordinary Shares: owners of ordinary shares have the right to vote at a company's Annual General Meeting and they receive a dividend declared by the Directors of the Company at the end of a financial year.

Preference Shares: owners of preference shares do not usually have the right to vote at a company's Annual General Meeting but receive a fixed rate of dividend which must be paid before any dividend is paid to Ordinary Shareholders.

Dividend: the directors of a company decide whether a dividend should be paid and the amount. The amount of the dividend depends on the amount of profit the company has earned in a financial year. A dividend is paid to a shareholder on every share owned and is always expressed in pence per share. If the dividend is 5p per share and a shareholder has 100 shares, a dividend of £5 is paid to that shareholder.

Nominal Value of a Share: this is the face value of a share issued by a company. A share with a nominal value of £1 will normally be sold by the company at that price on the formation of the Company.

The amount of **called up** Share Capital which appears in the Balance Sheet of a company will be quoted at nominal value, for example:

Share Capital
  Ordinary Shares 500,000 at £1 each: £500,000

Share Premium Account: a company may not issue all its authorized share capital when it is formed. If it is successful and earns a profit it may at a later date issue more shares and it will be able to sell these shares at a price in excess of the nominal value. This excess is termed the **share premium value**, and an account is maintained to record the amount. The balance on this account—the Share premium Account—appears as a separate entry in a Company's Balance Sheet.

Loan capital

Funds from an external source, such as a bank or debenture holders, which are committed to the firm on a long-term basis.

Despite being an external liability for the firm, the term capital is still applied to such loans because of the long-term nature of the commitment.

Capital expenditure

Expenditure on fixed assets or on the improvement of fixed assets in such a way as to increase their value. Expenditure is capitalized if its cost is included in the balance sheet and then subjected to depreciation procedures, rather than being simply charged to the manufacturing, trading, or profit and loss accounts for the period as revenue expenditure.

See also **Revenue expenditure**

Cash book

The cash book consists of a combination of the records of cash in hand and the current bank account of an organization. All receipts and payments related to cash or bank balances are recorded in the book, which forms part of the overall double-entry book-keeping system. It is a particularly important document in relation to the control of cash, and the reconciliation of records kept by the organization with those held by the bank. This reconciliation of the cash book balance with the bank statement is called a **bank reconciliation statement.**

Club accounts

Accounts of clubs, societies, and other non-profit making organizations are kept in a form similar to that used by commercial organizations. Although the format of the accounts is substantially the same, the titles change.

Commercial organization	*Club or society*
Cash book	Receipts and payments account
Trading account	Trading account
Profit and loss account	Income and expenditure account
Balance sheet	Statement of affairs

These accounts are normally kept by the club treasurer or drawn up by an accountant annually and then presented to the Annual General Meeting of the club for approval by the members.

Cost of goods sold

A figure calculated in the trading account of organizations by adjusting purchases for changes in stock levels.

$$\textbf{Cost of goods sold} = \textbf{Opening stock} + \textbf{Purchases} - \textbf{Closing stock}$$

This figure is then deducted from sales for the period to calculate gross profit.

Sales – Cost of goods sold = Gross profit

Cost accounting, costing

The branch of accounting which deals with the ascertainment, analysis, classification, and monitoring of costs in an organization. It is closely related to the use of budgets as financial targets and the monitoring of subsequent actual figures in order to compare them.

Cost behaviour

The classification of costs according to their values at different levels of activity. This classification forms the basis for the technique of break-even analysis.

Fixed costs are those which stay the same over a wide range of activity levels, such as rent, rates, or insurance.

Variable costs are those which vary in direct proportion to the activity level, such as direct materials, packaging costs, or machine power costs.

Semi-variable costs are those which contain elements of both fixed and variable costs. In most organizations electricity costs have a basic fixed element, relating to lighting and heating of the premises even during low activity periods, and a variable element relating to power used to run machinery. Overall the cost of electricity is said to be a semi-variable cost.

Stepped costs are those costs which are fixed for small ranges of activity level but which then change in a sudden discrete step. For example, a firm may find that it can operate with a simple delivery van up to about 30% of its normal activity level, but that when this level is exceeded another van must be used. Depreciation of these vans would be classified as stepped cost.

Relevant Cost

The cost that is necessary to ascertain when undertaking an investigation into the financial effects of a particular decision. Not all costs will be relevant in, for instance, a make-or-buy decision, where only the specific marginal costs of manufacture should be compared with the outside supplies price. This is a 'context related' cost in that what is related is very much dependent on the specific circumstances relating to a situation.

Opportunity Cost

The revenue or benefit foresaken as a result of undertaking a particular course of action. Often if there are competing demands for resources one particular activity may have to be foresaken and the potential revenue lost so that an alternative strategy can be adopted.

Sunk Cost

A cost already undertaken and the expenditure completed. For instance a machine purchased in the past may have a book value for accounting purposes. If a decision regarding replacement needs to be made this undepreciated book value is irrelevant, as the initial cost is a past or sunk cost.

Credit sales

Sales in which the goods or services are delivered but payment is delayed until a later date. The seller of the goods or services becomes a **creditor** of the person or organization to whom they are sold until payment is made.

Current ratio

A measure of the liquidity of an organization. The ratio compares the value of current assets with current liabilities to establish the ability of an organization to cover its short-term liabilities. It is usually interpreted in conjunction with the liquid assets ratio and is calculated as follows:

$$\textbf{Current ratio} = \frac{\textbf{Current assets}}{\textbf{Current liabilities}} : \textbf{1}$$

It is generally reckoned that the ratio should be a value of about 2 : 1. A much lower ratio indicates possible problems with meeting liabilities in a hurry, while a much higher ratio indicates that funds are not being used effectively.

Debenture

A loan made to a limited company in exchange for which a debenture certificate is issued and an annual fixed interest charge is paid. Although often confused with them, debentures are not shares and do not imply any ownership rights in the company. The certificates once issued may change hands at some market price, but this does not change the liability of the company. The liability of the company continues to be the amount of the original loan.

Debtor

A person or organization who owes money to another person or organization. The amount of the debt is shown as a current asset in the balance sheet of the person or organization to whom the money is owed. Debtors are treated as liquid assets when assessing the liquidity of an organization as they may be turned into cash quickly should the need arise. Debts of debtors who fail to pay are known as **bad debts**.

Depreciation

The term given to the reduction in book value of a fixed asset charged as an expense to the profit and loss account. It is not a transfer of funds but a non-cash book transfer which enables the cost of fixed assets to be spread evenly through their useful life. When the accumulated depreciation charged against an asset is deducted from the original cost, the remainder is known as the **book value**.

$$\textbf{Book value} = \frac{\textbf{original}}{\textbf{cost of asset}} - \frac{\textbf{accumulated depreciation}}{\textbf{already charged}}$$

The accumulated depreciation to date is shown as a deduction from the appropriate class of fixed assets in the balance sheet.

Discounting methods

A series of techniques for the appraisal of capital investment projects which evaluates costs and revenues taking into account the time value of money. Because money can earn interest over time, cash received sooner is worth more than cash received later. By taking into account the interest which earlier receipt could earn, or **discounting**, future costs and receipts may be expressed in **present value** terms, thus making easier comparison of competing projects. Such **discounted cash flow** techniques include the calculation of a percentage rate of return for a capital investment which takes into account the timing of all payments and receipts relating to the project. The percentage measure is known as the **internal rate of return**.

Expenses

Expenses, or business expenses, are costs charged against gross profit in the profit and loss account of an organization.

When deducted from gross profit, the remainder is net profit.

All expenses may be classified as overheads and are normally sub-divided into administrative expenses, selling and distribution expenses, and financial expenses. Financial expenses are interest charges and other costs directly related to the provision of external funds to finance the organization. The analysis, monitoring and control of expenses is one of the main functions of costs accounting.

Final accounts

The term referring to the accounts produced by an organization at the end of an accounting period in order to calculate profit or loss and then to update the balance sheet. The final accounts include a manufacturing account and trading account, a profit and loss account and, when appropriate, an end of period balance sheet. The equivalent accounts for a club or society or a public sector organization are also sometimes referred to as final accounts.

Fixed costs
See **Cost behaviour**

Gearing

Gearing is a term which relates fixed capital, such as preference shares, debentures, and other loans, with ordinary share capital, or equity capital, which attracts variable percentage dividends. A highly geared company is one with a high proportion of fixed interest capital, whereas a company with low gearing has a high proportion of ordinary share capital. Thus a highly geared company is committed to making a large amount of profit simply in order to cover interest payable on its fixed-interest finances.

Gross profit

Gross profit is the difference between sales revenue and cost of sales. It is the simple profit made from trading, representing the amount by which the trader has marked up goods purchased or manufactured before selling them. It is calculated in the trading account of an organization and represents profit before the deduction of business expenses.

Sales – Cost of sales = Gross profit
Gross profit – Expenses = Net profit

Gross profit as a percentage of sales

A measure of profitability expressing the proportion of a trader's turnover which is profit made from increasing the price of bought or manufacturing goods.

$$\text{Gross profit as a percentage of sales} = \frac{\text{Gross profit}}{\text{Sales}} \times 100\%$$

This measure is sometimes referred to as the **gross margin**. As a single measure it has little meaning and must be compared with previous percentages made by organizations undertaking similar business activities.

Income and expenditure accounts
See **Club accounts**

Interpretation of accounts

The techniques of deriving meaning from accounting statements. By examining the accounts and calculating accounting ratios which measure profitability, liquidity and activity, an assessment can be made of the financial performance and status of an organization during an accounting period and at any given time. When interpreting accounts, three comparisons are normally possible:

a Comparison with absolute or generally accepted values for certain ratios, such as the recommended 1 : 1 level for the liquid assets ratio.
b Comparison with the performance of the same organization during other accounting periods, thus showing changes and trends in the performance of the organization.
c Comparison with other similar organizations.

Insolvency

The condition when the external liabilities of an organization exceed its assets, leading to a negative capital figure on the balance sheet. It is an offence for a business or company to trade when knowingly insolvent. When creditors make claims in law against such a business or company it may lead to bankruptcy and liquidation respectively.

Liquid assets ratio (*also known as* **Acid test ratio** *or* **Quick assets ratio)**

A liquidity ratio which compares current liabilities with the funds which might easily be made available to meet them.

$$\textbf{Liquid assets ratio} = \frac{\textbf{Current assets } \textit{less} \textbf{ stock}}{\textbf{Current liabilities}} : 1$$

It is generally recommended that the value of this ratio should be about 1 : 1. If it is much higher than this, funds are not being used to best advantage. If it is significantly lower than 1 : 1, the organization may have difficulty in meeting current liabilities quickly, should the need arise.

Liquidity ratios

Accounting ratios designed to indicate the current status of an organization in relation to its external liabilities and its ability to meet its debts if required. The main liquidity ratios are the **current ratio** and the **liquid assets ratio**. Liquid funds are those which are most like cash in that they are easily exchangeable for goods or services.

Mortgage

A loan provided to an individual or organization which is secured against a specific property, normally a house or other building. The lender has first claim to the property in the event of a default on the loan, bankruptcy of the individual borrower, or liquidation of a borrowing company.

Net present value

A term relating to discounting techniques for project appraisal. The net present value of revenue is its value taking into account all costs, with both costs and revenues having been discounted to take account of the time value of money. If the net present value of a project is positive at a given rate of discount, this indicates that the project is producing a percentage rate of a return higher than the discount rate.

Net profit

The residual revenue for a period after taking into account all costs. It is calculated in the profit and loss account at the end of an accounting period by deducting expenses from gross profit.

Net profit = Gross profit *less* Expenses

It is regarded as an extremely important measure of an organization's performance in that it measures its earnings for the period after having met all expenses. It is the figure on which the tax liability for a business is calculated.

Net profits as a percentage of capital employed (*also known as* **return on capital employed**)

A profitability ratio which measures the earnings of an organization in relation to the funds which it is using.

$$\textbf{Net profit as a percentage of capital employed} = \frac{\textbf{Net profit}}{\textbf{Capital employed}} \times 100\%$$

The capital employed figure used should be an average of capital employed at the start of the year and that at year end. Calculation of this ratio is further complicated if interest on long-term loans has been deducted when calculating net profit. In this case, such interest should be added back into net profit before making the calculation. Once calculated, the percentage should compare favourably with that earned by capital elsewhere. For example, if a similar amount were placed on deposit in a bank, a rate close to the bank rate could be earned with minimal risk. Thus a commercial, risk-taking, organization will normally expect to produce a return on capital employed in excess of such a percentage.

Net profit as a percentage of sales

A performance ratio which expresses the profit margin of an organization after taking into account all costs.

$$\textbf{Net profit as a percentage of sales} = \frac{\textbf{Net profit}}{\textbf{Sales}} \times \textbf{100\%}$$

Such a measure has no meaning on its own but is useful when compared with previous performances of the same organization or with other organizations of a similar nature. It is often read in conjunction with **gross profit as a percentage of sales** to indicate the extent to which expenses reduce the margins being earned in trading.

Operating statement
See **Profit and loss account**

Overheads

A term given to those costs which are neither direct material, direct labour, nor direct expense costs. They are operating expenses of the business and their cost behaviour may be either as fixed costs or variable costs. In terms of management control they are often the target for special attention since they may, if not carefully managed, account for a disproportionately high amount of the organization's costs. One cost accounting technique of **full absorption costing** will require all overhead costs to be allocated or apportioned to specific parts of the business operation so that these costs can be spread into the cost of individual jobs or units of production.

Payback period

A method of evaluating investment projects which assesses the time which it takes for cash inflows to pay back the initial cash outflows on an investment. Organizations often prefer projects with a short payback period, and the technique may be used as a method of sifting out those projects which take a particularly long time to pay back, remaining projects being ranked by other means. As a sole method of project appraisal, its biggest disadvantage is that it ignores all returns beyond the payback date.

Prepayments

Expenses paid for in advance of the accounting period to which they refer. Some expenses, such as rates and insurance, are generally payable in advance. Because of the accounting principle of matching revenue and cost for a period, advance payments are not counted against profit in the expenses figure used in the profit and loss account. Instead the amount paid in advance appears in the balance sheet as a current asset, as the organization is owed a service by the person or organization to whom the prepayment was made.

Profit and loss account

Part of the final accounts of an organization drawn up at the end of each accounting period. The profit and loss account starts with the gross profit and deducts business expenses in order to establish the net profit. A version of the profit and loss account is sometimes called an **operating statement**. The equivalent account in the case of a club or society is known as an **income and expenditure account**.

Profitability

The extent to which an organization makes satisfactory earnings from its operations. Net profit, and in some cases gross profit, is compared with other figures in order to assess the performance of the organization. The main ratios measuring profitability are **gross profit as a percentage of sales, net profit as a percentage of sales** and **net profit as a percentage of capital employed**.

Quick assets ratio
See **Liquid assets ratio**

Rate of stock turnover

An activity ratio which measures the speed at which an organization sells its stock.

$$\textbf{Rate of stock turnover} = \frac{\textbf{Cost of sales}}{\textbf{Average stock}}$$

This rate indicates the number of times in a given period that the shelves are notionally cleared. A fast rate of stock turnover means that the gross profit margin is being achieved on more occasions in each accounting period. When read in conjunction with the gross profit as a percentage of sales ratio, it indicates a style of trading. Some businesses aim to achieve a large margin on each sale, even if this means that sales are relatively infrequent (high margin, slow turnover), whereas others are happy to make a small profit on each of a large number of sales (low margin, fast turnover).

Ratio analysis

A technique used in the interpretation of accounts which makes comparisons between figures in a given set of accounts, or between the same figure in various sets of accounts, in order to judge the financial performance of the organization. The main groupings of ratios are **activity ratios, liquidity ratios,** and **profitability ratios**.

Return on capital employed
See **Net profit as percentage of capital employed**

Revaluation reserve

A company may revalue its Fixed Assets based on current market value. When an asset is revalued, the asset account is debited with the difference between the market price of the asset and the original cost of the asset. This difference is credited to a Revaluation Account or Revlance Reserve Account and appears as a Liability in the Balance Sheet.

Revenue account

This is an account which shows the income and expenditure of a non-profit making organization such as a local authority. It shows the day-to-day expenditure on such items as salaries and wages, and income received in the form of government grants, rents, and charges.

The Revenue Account is used to calculate whether the organization has made a **surplus** or a **deficit** on its activities in a financial year.

Revenue expenditure

Day-to-day expenses of an organization which are charged to the revenue accounts (manufacturing, trading and profit and loss accounts) for the period in which they occur. In contrast **capital expenditure** is the expenditure on fixed assets which are expected to be used within the organization for some considerable time in the future.

Sales to capital employed

An activity ratio which relates the amount of business transacted by an organization to the amount of funds invested in it.

$$\textbf{Sales to capital employed} = \frac{\textbf{Sales}}{\textbf{Capital employed}}$$

There is no set level for such a ratio, but it may be monitored in order to trace trends of activity within an organization or else to compare it with the ratios of similar organizations.

Semi-variable costs
See **Cost behaviour**

Share capital

This may be sub-divided as follows:

Authorized capital: The amount of funds which may be supplied to a company in exchange for part ownership as defined in the memorandum and articles of association.

Issued share capital: Funds actually supplied by the shareholders and used for the purchase of assets to enable business to take place. The capital may be contrasted with **loan capital** which is provided from sources other than the owners of the company.

Standard accountancy practice

An agreed set of principles and conventions which enables accountants to communicate effectively with one another, and to give a true and fair view of the financial affairs of an organization. Details of the accepted practice are contained in a series of **Statements of Standard Accountancy Practice** (SSAP) which provide concise guidelines on formats, principles and conventions. *See* **Accounting concepts and conventions**.

Stepped costs
See **Cost behaviour**

Stock

Stock is the name given by a firm to goods held which it subsequently hopes to sell or to convert into a saleable product. In a trading organization it consists simply of goods bought for resale. In a manufacturing concern, it may refer to raw materials, work in progress, or finished goods. In all cases stock should be valued at cost or market value, whichever is the lower, in accordance with the accounting convention of prudence.

Stock-turn ratio
See **Rate of stock turnover**

Trading account

An account which forms part of the group of financial statements called the **final accounts**; it summarizes transactions for an accounting period. The trading account is used for the calculation of gross profit by deducting cost of goods sold from sales. The equation of the trading account is:

Sales *less* Cost of goods sold = Gross profit

Cost of goods sold is found by applying a stock adjustment to purchases:

Opening stock *add* Purchases *less* Closing stock = Cost of goods sold

The trading account follows the manufacturing account and precedes the profit and loss account in the final accounts.

Variable costs
See **Cost behaviour**

Index